Postmarked Ever After

By

Mary L. Ball

Dedicated to all those who have grieved the loss of someone dear and found the courage to love again.

All scriptures references taken from the King James Bible

CHAPTER ONE

AS DARKNESS APPROACHED, Serena scanned the boxes scattered throughout her new condominium. Silently, she thanked the

Lord the movers had delivered her furniture earlier.

In the glow from a lamp light, the torn, crinkled envelope she laid on the mantle caught her eye and pulled her towards it-like fireflies to a flame. Serena reached for the letter and took a seat near the window. She gazed out at the sky covered with stars, flickering like jewels. In slow motion, she opened the envelope and scanned the familiar page for the hundredth time. Serena rubbed her tired shoulders and read the words as she drifted to sleep.

THE DOORBELL RANG. Serena rubbed her neck and rose from the sofa. She arched her back trying to stretch out the kinks from an uncomfortable night. A quick glance at the clock reminder her that her friend offered to help unpack. She grabbed the letter and laid it on the mantel then stepped over a carton marked nick-knacks as she made her way to the door.

"Betsy, did you have a good trip?" Serena moved aside and motioned for her to enter.

"Yes, I did." Betsy stepped inside and looked around. "The traffic was hectic in Wilmington, but once I got on Interstate 421, it was fine. Serena, this is a lovely place. The Wood Shake Shingles are nice." She walked through the space and peeked in the rooms.

"It is pretty and from the dining area you can walk out onto the patio." Serena led her toward the glass doors.

They stepped into the kitchen. Her friend turned and surveyed the area. "Wow, I like your new home." She opened a cabinet and looked inside. A stainless-steel storage bin caught her eye, "How nice, you have a vegetable sink."

"I know it's a great feature, and I'm going to enjoy the dark hardwoods." She eyed the floor and then reached in the refrigerator. "I know you only drink coffee in the wee hours of the morning." Serena handed Betsy a cola.

"Yes, I had my fill of java before I left home. I see you've been unpacking." She motioned toward a half-empty box on the counter.

"Yeah, I started yesterday after the movers left"

"Since you began in the kitchen, I'll help you get the rest of the dishes put away." Betsy popped the tab on her cola and took a sip.

The two best friends worked throughout the day emptying boxes and placing household items in their designated spot. Serena picked up a flyer she gotten from a pasta restaurant,

"Let's have Pizza for dinner. How's that sound to you?"

"Great, and after we eat, we can work some more. You know what kind I like" Betsy watched as Serena placed the call in for the order.

Hours later, Serena and Betsy smoothed the comforter on the bed in the guest. Betsy opened her suitcase and took out her PJ's. "I'm tired, but we got a lot of unpacking done today." She sat on the bed.

Serena nodded and glanced at the clock on the bedside table. "It would have taken me weeks to get everything sorted without your help." She took a seat in the armchair next to the doorway.

"Do you plan to clean out any more boxes tonight?" Betsy leaned back on her hands.

"No, I'm calling it quits for now. It's been a long day."

Betsy looked around the bedroom. "Are you glad you moved to Greensboro?"

"Yeah, I need to be closer to Mom. When her doctor told me she was in the early stages of Alzheimer's I wanted to move so I could to spend more time with her. I was lucky Long Pine Regional Hospital had a nurse's position open. I'm going to enjoy working in the Pediatrics wing." Serena pushed her hair back. "But relocating is harder than I thought, especially when you're by yourself."

The room grew quiet. Serena's mind wondered to the days before Jason's accident. She recalled the words her beloved had spoken many times. Serena, my work can get dangerous. I love you, but you must promise not to be afraid to seek happiness if something happens to me.

The things he said hurt at the time, but now they gave her comfort. Serena leaned her head back against the chair, reliving that horrible night she'd received word of her husband's death. If only he hadn't gone into that alley.

Betsy yawned as she watched Serena. "Hey, you're a million miles away."

"I guess this move has me contemplating life. I never figured Jason could get hurt. Why would anyone shoot a Criminal Investigator for delving into a financial felony? This is the first time since college I've relocated anywhere without him." Serena shook her head trying to clear her thoughts. "He's been gone for two years, it's still hard at times."

"I know it must be." Betsy looked down at the bed covering; she longed to find comforting words, but found herself at a loss. "You're a strong woman. Remember you're not alone. The

Lord's a prayer away, and I'm a phone call from you."

"My strength has come from God's word." Serena grinned, "And I do appreciate your friendship." She stood and walked to the door. I'll see you in the morning.

Serena moved down the hallway and stepped into the living room to close the blinds. Once more, she saw the crinkled envelope. She sighed and reached for the letter. Many times, she'd started to toss it in the trash, but she couldn't seem to part with it yet. She stared at the faded words.

March 12, 2011

Dear Jason,

Please forgive me for writing you this way with the news I must share; I should have told you long ago. I think back to our school days. I thought I could care for you, but when Adam and I put our differences aside, I knew he was my future. I've always loved Adam; however, you have a special place in my heart.

Jason, do you remember when we went to the lake?

What seemed like true love that day...?

I found out three months later, how those few hours could change a person's life forever. I wanted to contact you then, tell you, but you had gone away to college. I married Adam right away, and relied on God's forgiveness for what happened between us.

For years, I debated contacting you, always waiting until tomorrow, but it was never the right time. Last month, I found out I don't have many tomorrows left. I'm dying. I have terminal Cancer. I'm grateful for God's forgiveness, but I must also undo a wrong.

With your parents retired and living in Hawaii, I didn't know how to contact you, but I ran into one of your mother's friends and she gave me the last known address she had.

Jason, I can't go on to be with the Lord without letting you know that you have a daughter. Her name is Nicky. Please remember, although she is your biological child, she loves Adam, and he loves her very much. Adam has raised her as though she were his child. Along with getting to know Nicky, I'm asking you to let Adam continue to be part of her life also.

Forgive me, Katie

Serena wiped a tear and slipped the note back into the envelope. Her body shook with emotion as the tears fell. Minutes later, she fixed her eyes on a small framed picture that sat on top of a carton. Her lips curled in a slight grin. "I always did like that little brown beauty mark you had above your upper lip." She exhaled. "You have a daughter Jason. I wonder if she looks like you."

Serena walked to the window, closed the blinds, and picked up the picture. "If only you had known a child was produced from that high school fling." As she put the photo back, she couldn't help but wonder why Katie didn't contact Jason years earlier.

THE NEXT DAY SERENA drove Betsy to a fast-food restaurant. They enjoyed a simple breakfast and headed back to the condominium to begin the task of unpacking more boxes. They both worked with determination, and late that afternoon the women walked from one room to another.

"Gee, Betsy we made a lot of progress. Almost all the cartons are empty."

Betsy agreed and followed behind Serena as they eyed into each room. "I think the spare bedrooms are the only places left that have moving containers to clear out."

"Yes, the living room looks great and the place finally feels like home. Since you're leaving in the morning, let's just relax tonight."

"Okay, if you're sure," Betsy laughed. "I don't want to go out anywhere. Let's stay in and watch a movie."

"I've been so busy unpacking. I forgot to stock food." Serena tapped a finger on her lip.

"You know I like take-out, go get us something," Betsy shooed her on.

Serena gathered her pocketbook and pointed to the remote. "You find a movie for us to watch, what do you want to eat?"

"Chicken strips." Betsy's voice rang out as she turned on the television.

SERENA PULLED OFF HOLDEN Road into the parking lot of Chicken Fingers. She moved the rear-view mirror and smoothed her hair, then applied lip-gloss. She walked into the restaurant and glanced around at the crowded room. Taking a few steps, Serena paused beside a table reading the large menu that hung above the checkout counter.

"Excuse me." A voice drew her attention.

Serena looked at the man as he pushed himself out of a booth and extended his hand toward the table. "I'm leaving if

you would like this seat. I think it's the only one vacant now"

She stared at the man. The words eye candy popped in her head. Serena smiled at the handsome face in front of her. He was at least six inches taller than she, with a dimple in his chin. Excitement crawled to the surface; her heart pounded. With a quick glance, his brown eyes mesmerized her. "Thanks, but I'm ordering take-out."

Mr. Eye Candy flashed pearly whites her way. "I recommend the breaded honey mustard chicken." He nodded and

began to walk away. "Have a nice evening."

She watched him go. A waitress approached and Serena requested, "Two orders of the breaded honey mustard fingers please."

AS SERENA CARRIED THE food into the condominium, she overheard Betsy say goodbye to someone on her cell phone. "Betsy, I'm sorry. I've taken your time this weekend I know you have a lot of planning to do for your wedding."

"I do, but I wanted to help. Keith will survive without me a few days. And don't forget, we have to shop for your bride's maid dress next month."

"I would never overlook my best friend's wedding. I'll try to get a schedule worked out with a weekend off to go to Wilmington, so we can shop for your big day."

"Here." Serena held a Styrofoam box out to Betsy.

They walk into the kitchen together. Once seated, both women bowed their heads. "Lord, I ask you to bless the food. I thank you for being with me on this move and I petition you

to guide my friends as they embark in matrimony."

Betsy chimed in with an "Amen."

While they ate, the upcoming wedding was their first topic. Serena took a bite of chicken. "It's as delicious as he said."

Betsy stopped chewing. "What? Who said?"

"The chicken, Mr. Eye Candy said it was good." Serena took another bite of the food.

Her friend laughed. "Who in the world has a name like that?"

Serena wiped her hands on a napkin and smiled. "I doubt that's his name, but it's what I've decided to call him. He offered me his seat as he was leaving the restaurant." She picked up another strip of chicken, "Best looking man I've seen in a long time, and he suggested this yummy chicken."

Betsy eyed Serena. "Did you get his number?"

"No silly, I couldn't just say, Hey what's your number, you good looking thing." Serena enhanced her southern drawl and laughter filled the air. "He's probably married anyway."

When Betsy rose to help Serena clear the table she added, "Well at least Greensboro, North Carolina has possibilities."

They walked to the living room. "Serena, I saw that letter on your side table. I thought you threw it away months ago."

"When I packed things from my desk, I found it. I wish I'd never seen it. I remember Jason mentioning the woman to me before we married. Since Jason and I didn't have any children, he would have been happy to know he had a child. It makes me mad. First, he died in a horrible accident, and then I find out a woman from his past kept his baby from him."

Betsy admired her friend's earrings as they talked. The heart shaped gold held a square ruby in the middle. If her memory was correct, they were the last gift Serena received from her husband before his accident. "There's nothing you can do about that letter or something that happened thirteen years ago between Jason and a high school girl friend."

A tentative grin crossed Serena's lips, "You're right. I considered searching for his child, but I couldn't, even if I wanted. You know how battered the envelope is. The return address is

unreadable, besides it doesn't matter now. Jason is gone."

THE NEXT MORNING SERENA said good-bye to her friend. "I know we worked hard, but it was fun. Thanks for all your help. Are you sure you can get back to Wilmington?"

"Piece of cake," Betsy lifted her hand in the air as if batting Serena's concerns away. They hugged goodbye. As Betsy drove away, Serena waved.

CHAPTER TWO

AS SPRING DREW CLOSER, Serena settled into her new position at Long Pine Hospital. When the schedule allowed, she attended church not far from home.

Early morning rain poured as Serena rushed from her car to the hospital entrance. She stepped on the elevator and exited on the fourth floor. After logging onto the computer, she organized the charts, and started making rounds.

Clovers and Leprechauns embellished the walls of the children's wing. Serena wore green, being forewarned by a redhaired six-year-old if she didn't wear the right color for Saint's Patrick's Day, she could get pinched. Serena smiled as began her day. She always enjoyed children. Being around them in the children's ward was good even when things didn't work out the way she wished it did. She'd liked how the kids were optimistic. Even where their illness seemed dim, they showed happiness.

The kids brighten my life.

"Hi Serena," Carole opened the employee program in the computer and typed her time in for the day.

"Morning, Carole." She looked over the charts. "We have a new patient." Serena pointed to the clipboard

"Yes, the boy was brought into the ER last night. His name is Dillon Washington. He has Long QT Syndrome."

Serena pressed her lips together. "That explains the chaotic heartbeats."

Carole agreed, "It's a good thing he passed out. The child's condition could have gone unnoticed. His parents said he started playing basketball at the YMCA and that's what triggered it, Dillon is lucky. It's sad; we've seen too many people die

with this condition before it could be treated."

Serena closed the file. "You're right, it's a blessing."

"Want to join me for lunch. I made a pot roast last night and we had leftovers. I brought enough for two." Carole started to walk away and turned back to ask.

"Sure, that sounds great." Serena nodded she could already taste lunch.

Time sped as she tended the young patients. When Serena stepped behind the nurse's desk, she noticed the swinging tail of the big cat clock that hung over the counter. The black paws on twelve reminded Serena it was her lunchtime.

She went to the restroom and then stepped in the eating lounge. While she waited for Carole, Serena called her mother.

"Mom, how are you doing today?"

"Serena," her mother's voice rose in excitement. "It's good to hear from you, when are you coming to see me?"

"I'm coming in a few days. We'll enjoy lunch together."

"Oh, that's wonderful. You can tell me all about your new place."

"I will. I'd better go, I'll call you later. Mom, I love you."

"I love you," her mom's voice cracked with age as she hesitated, "too dear."

Carole walked in the room as Serena ended the call and began dishing out roast on paper plates. "How's your mother doing?"

Serena grabbed a bottle of water out of the refrigerator. "She's doing as well as expected. I've visited her several times since I've moved here, but she still talks like I've only been in town a few days."

"It's difficult when anyone's memory starts to fade." Carole set the food down in front of Serena and took a seat. Both women bowed their heads as Carole prayed.

Serena forked a bite of roast and chewed, savoring the spicy taste. "Umm..., this is good, Carole. You're such a wonderful cook."

"It comes from years of having to feed a man." She glanced at Serena and noticed a slight wrinkle come on her face at the remark. "I'm sorry. I forgot about your husband." "it's okay, Carole." She sipped water.

"You're a brave lady, moving and starting over." "I like it here." Serena glanced around the room.

"Well, we're glad you're on staff."

"Thanks, Carole. I appreciate you inviting me to Sunday service. I dislike having to start at a new church alone."

"I'm glad you enjoyed it, I've gone there for fifteen years."

"It's a lovely worship center. I enjoyed meeting the people there, and Pastor Bob's sermon Sunday was enlightening. It's funny, but at times certain verses in the Bible mean more than they ever did before."

Carole smiled, "I know. I've found that God's word ministers to me as my needs change."

"I'm certainly going to continue to attend when my work schedules permit." She shrugged apologetically.

"Pastor Bob knows people have careers that require working Sundays. He told me that when God gave his children a desire to work in a field different from the Monday to Friday routine, He had a good reason. Our continued relationship with the Lord is the most important part of being a Christian." Carole stood and tossed the leftovers in the trash bin. "I wonder if you could help me out with something."

"I'll try, what's up." Serena rose from her chair.

"I promised the middle school that I would talk to one of the classes about nursing. At the time, I didn't realize it was the day I planned to be off. I have several things scheduled, one being a much-needed beauty shop appointment." Carole touched her hair. "Could you possibly go in my place and speak to the students?"

Serena contemplated. "If you need me, I will."

"Thanks Serena it's scheduled for Friday. I'll give you all the details tomorrow."

The day was busy, but before Serena left, she stopped by the new patient, Dillon's room. Several bright-colored balloons decorated the area. A cartoon played on the television. Serena walked to the side of the bed and adjusted the monitor. She grinned at the young patient, remembering from his records that he was around eleven years old.

"Hi Dillon," Serena took his temperature as he stared at her with wide eyes. She shook the thermometer. "You seem to be doing fine today."

Dillon watched the nurse. In his mind, he could still see the two people who spoke to him. He recalled a man mentioning that a nurse with brown hair would come to his room, and she would be wearing heart-shaped earrings with a square red stone.

"That man said you would be here."

"Was it the doctor?" She smiled at the child as she wrote on his chart.

"No, I saw him the night I came to the hospital. It was before they took me to a room. The man told me to tell you to start at the beginning."

Serena stopped noting vitals and stared at the boy. She nibbled at her bottom lip. For reasons she couldn't explain chilly goose bumps pricked her arms. She listened to the child and tried to remember which medication may have caused Dillon to think he saw or heard someone other than the staff while he was in the emergency room.

She cleared her throat, "Did you say, he told you to give me a message, about a beginning?"

Dillon shook his head, "I saw two people standing in a meadow. I've never seen the grass that bright green before." The boy's voice rose. "He even told me you would be wearing heart earrings. The woman with him said, the beginning is where you'll find a happy ending, and everything will be okay. The lady had real long hair and she was smiling."

The boy's words rang in her ears. She swallowed hard and touched one of the earrings. Serena could hardly believe what she was hearing. "Dillon, do you remember what this man looked like?"

"He was older than my dad, fatter too. He had a round brown mark under his nose."

She stepped back and put her hand to her chest when the boy mentioned the birthmark. "Think hard, is there anything else you can tell me?"

Without looking up, he shook his head. "Both of them said something about trusting Jesus and having faith in your heart.

That's all I remember."

Dillon turned his attention away from to the television and looked at Serena. "I saw Heaven didn't I? It was kinda like some of the pictures I've seen in my Bible story book, only brighter."

She patted his hand. "Dillon, thank you for telling me, I'd better go." Serena retreated from the room and leaned against the wall to steady her nerves before she left for home.

SERENA STORED HER TOTE in the closet and walked to the kitchen. She glanced out of the window and stared at the privacy fence in the backyard, her mind still on the day's events. She turned on the CD player. A fast rhythm of piano and guitar music filled the room as a female's voice sang a southern gospel song.

Serena opened a can and began to fix chicken noodle soup. After she poured her meal in a bowl and sat, she grabbed the phone and called Betsy. The recorder instructed her to leave a message. She responded, asking her friend to call as soon as possible. An hour later, her phone buzzed.

"Hi Serena, is everything okay? You said it was important." Betsy's voice sounded concerned

"You're not going to believe what happened." Serena hurried to get the words out. "I was making rounds and a new patient came in early this morning. The things he said."

Serena rehashed the conversation she had with Dillon in the young patient's room. "The boy even pointed out the earrings I had on. I was trying to dismiss it, until he spoke about Jason's birthmark."

"I've heard about things like this happening, I never knew anyone who experienced it. What will you do?"

"Um… Take a hot bath and think." She attempted a chuckle, and then blew out a shaky breath. "Nothing, it's just so odd. Anyway, it could be a number of things; maybe the boy has a big imagination." She changed the subject, "Have you made any more wedding plans?"

"Keith and I finally agreed on a date. We decided September twenty-fifth."

"That's wonderful. I'm so happy for you. I'm sorry we had to cancel the dress shopping, but I have it all worked out now. In three weeks, I can come on Friday and stay until Sunday morning."

Serena and Betsy chatted about dresses. While they spoke, Serena unloaded the dryer and headed to the bedroom with a few clothes to fold.

"I emailed you some photos to look at."

"You did? Let me see." Serena trotted to the computer and opened the email. "I like the outfit enhanced with beads, the one with the Basque waistline and lacey off the shoulder sleeves."

"I figured you would. It's pretty, but I may choose the silk taffeta with spaghetti straps, the train isn't as long, fewer chances of me tripping" Betsy chuckled.

"That's a pretty dress too-it'll look fantastic on you. You're not going to stumble while going down the aisle."

"Serena, when you come to Wilmington? We can go over the decorations to match the colors I've chosen."

"You've picked your colors?"

"Yeah, I've always like Sapphire, and yellow together."

Serena closed her laptop. "Those are great colors for a fall wedding. Make notes and we'll go over everything when I get to your house."

Serena pressed end on her phone and smiled at the excitement she'd heard in her friend's voice.

FRIDAY AFTERNOON SERENA straightened her scrubs while she walked through the main entrance of South Gilman Middle School. She made her way to the office and secured a visitor pass and directions to Ms. Hardy eight-grade class. As Serena entered, the teacher stood and welcomed her.

"Class, this is Ms. Gray, she's a pediatric nurse from Long Pine Regional Hospital. Ms. Gray is going to share with us the responsibilities of working in a hospital. Maybe she'll give us some examples of her daily activities." The teacher glanced toward Serena. "Thank you for coming, we look forward to learning a little about what it takes to become a hospital caregiver."

Serena leaned her tote bag, full of pamphlets for the students, against the podium. She smiled at the twenty sets of eyes staring in her direction, took a deep breath, and began her speech.

"As you know, I'm Serena Gray. Becoming a nurse is the most rewarding thing I've done." For a minute, her mind scanned back to her college days and the reports she gave in front of her class as she began to highlight the education needed for her field. She continued to speak about the degrees required for various other positions in nursing.

While she spoke, her eyes scanned the faces of the eighth graders. She didn't notice the man who stepped inside the door and stood watching. She turned her notes over and spotted a young girl seated in the last desk. The teenager's face looked distantly familiar.

Serena ended her discussion just as the bell rang for the students to change classes. She finished with, "I hope everyone learned something about the medical profession." Several of the students nodded encouragingly.

The man near the door walked out as the classes began to change. The teacher raised her voice above the ruckus of the students' gathering books and making their way to the hallway. "If anyone has questions for Ms. Gray, come up to the front?"

Ms. Hardy saw some students' approach. "I think a few in the class have comments Ms. Gray."

Serena smiled at the eager students. A boy inquired about anesthesiologists. Serena answered his question. A girl waited behind him and then approached. "Is it hard to watch someone die?" The student scrunched up her face.

"Yes, it's difficult." Serena inhaled and silently petitioned the Lord to help her answer. "As a nurse, we all do the best we can to care for people, but sometimes even the doctors can't help. The nice thing is we are there to offer comfort. Nursing is an important job and often the hospital staff are the only reassurance a family member has that someone cares."

After Serena's response, she watched the student who waited last, step closer. The teenager with the beauty mark over her lip was clad in embellished jeans.

"Ms. Gray, my name is Nicky."

"Nicky, that's a cute name." As Serena looked at the young lady she thought of the letter. The same name was scripted on the page from her husband's high school girlfriend.

The girl grinned shyly. "I was wondering – if I wanted to go to nursing school is there one close by? Course, I need to graduate first, but then I think I would like to become a nurse."

"Yes, there's a nice college in Greensboro with a very good nursing program."

The girl shrugged her shoulder. "I told my friend there was. She said I would have to go away to college to become a nurse. I don't want to leave home." Her voice aired a sadder tone. Nicky adjusted the books in her arms. "Thanks, it's really nice to talk with a nurse."

"You're welcome." As Nicky started to leave, she decided that she wanted to find out more about the adolescent who reminded her of someone and quickly offered, "Nicky here's my email address. Please, if you have any questions, you can write me." Serena jotted down her address and handed it to the teenager. "What's your last name?"

"It's Nicky Knox, Thanks Ms. Gray."

"You're welcome. I'll look forward to your emails."

Serena walked out of the room, satisfied that some students showed interest in the nursing profession. Her mind reeled with thoughts of Nicky. She resembled Jason some, but lots of people have birthmarks. She shook her head. No, it is too mind-boggling to think of such impossible nonsense. Jason had lived in New Jersey before he went to college and they married.

She walked down the hall toward the entrance of the school. Suddenly, a man stepped out of a doorway and greeted her.

"You must be the nurse who spoke to Ms. Hardy's class." He eyed Serena. At about the same time, they pointed a finger at each other and said, "Chicken Fingers."

Mr. Eye Candy laughed. "It's nice to see you again. Did you enjoy your meal?"

"I did. The food is wonderful and I ordered the honey mustard you recommended." Serena stared into his brown eyes.

"Do you work here?"

"I'm the principal. I appreciate you sharing with the students about the medical profession. My name is Adam Knox." He extended his hand.

She noticed that he scanned her left hand for a ring and she was sure her heart would stop when he mentioned his name. She pushed her lips together before commenting. "It's nice to meet you Mr. Knox. Do you have a daughter in Ms. Hardy's class?"

"Yes, and call me Adam" He looked at Serena, try as he might, he couldn't wipe the smile from his face. His eyes went to her heart shaped lips. He tried to look away, but she fascinated him.

Adam never dreamed he would see the beautiful woman from the restaurant again. His fingers itched to reach out and touch her. "My daughter was excited when she heard you were coming. A few years ago, we suffered a loss and since then she's shown an interest in nursing. Next year, Nicky will be a freshman in high school. It's good for her to be interested in future goals."

"It certainly is and you can call me Serena. You and your wife must be proud."

Serena watched the smile fade from Adam's face and he lowered his head toward the floor. "Her mother passed away two years ago."

"I'm sorry. Please accept my condolences." Serena wanted to say more, but she knew that at times like these there wasn't always comfort in words.

"Thank-you," Adam whispered.

"Adam, I don't mean to pry, but what was your wife's name?"

He looked at her and a slight grin returned to his face. "Katie."

Serena stopped a gasp from sounding and cleared her throat. For the second time today, her letter hovered in her mind. "I met Nicky today and I hope you don't mind, but I told her she could contact me by email anytime. She acted like she wanted to know more about the medical field."

"Not at all, thanks for reaching out to her. It'll be good for her to have an adult to talk to." Adam smiled. "I mean a female, that is." He swiped his hair. "Can I email you too? In case Nicky has a complicated question?"

"Sure." Serena pulled one of the hospital's business cards from her tote. Her hand shook as she scribbled her phone number and email address on the back.

Adam stuck the contact information in his pocket. "I'm glad you came to school and I got to properly meet you," he smiled wider. "I'll email you. Maybe, we can go out to Chicken Fingers together sometime?" He flashed a big smile. "That sounds like a lovely idea."

Serena strolled to the parking lot. The wind kicked up and blew the cloth tote swinging from her arm. Without thought, she grabbed the bag to secure it and opened her car door.

Lord, what am I going to do? Nicky, Adam, Katie. I'm not sure. She back out of the parking lot and pondered. Before she pulled into traffic, she scanned the clouds. "This is North Carolina, it's only a coincidence."

"HE'S TALL, HAS THICK hair and eyes that draw you in." Serena paced back and forth, as she chatted with Betsy.

"It sounds as if you like the guy."

"I don't know him but he's good looking and polite. What's not to like? Then I discovered a woman named Katie used to be his wife! From what he says, she died right after I lost Jason. I don't understand any of this. Could it be possible that it's the same family?"

"Well... you know they say it's a small world. You need to find out more. Are you going to show him the letter?"

"I can't say anything unless, I'm sure. But I am curious about him and his daughter." Serena twirled a piece of hair around her finger. "What if Jason is Nicky's real dad? How will Adam feel about finding that out?"

"Maybe you can ask him over for coffee and gently approach the subject. That's something only you can decide." Betsy lowered her voice. "I know it must be hard. I've got to go, talk to you soon."

Serena set down the phone, reached for the remote and clicked off the television, and then went to her bedroom. She opened her top dresser drawer and pulled out a gown.

Her eyes fell on a picture of Jason taken years earlier. "Jason, what do I do? What would you want me to do?"

Serena knelt in front of the bench at the foot of her bed. "Heavenly Father, if it's the same family do I tell Adam about my letter? I don't want to ruin anyone's life. Guide me Lord to do the right thing. In Jesus name, Amen."

CHAPTER THREE

ADAM AND NICKY SAT at the kitchen table. Adam watched Nicky scooped out a spoon full of macaroni and cheese.

"Did you enjoy listening to that nurse in class today?"

"Yes, she seems nice. She gave me her email address."

"Ms. Gray told me. She said you can email her anytime."

"She's pretty, Dad."

"Yes, she is." Adam took a bite from his pork chop.

During the meal, Nicky updated Adam on her day. He listened and gave a few encouraging words. When they were finished, the chair scrapped across the floor as Nicky scooted back and took her plate to the sink.

"You go upstairs and finish your homework. I've got the dishes." Adam placed leftovers in the refrigerator.

"Dad, it's your day to do dishes anyway." She giggled and kissed him on the cheek.

Adam watched as Nicky trotted up the steps toward her room. He rinsed a bowl to go into the dishwasher. His mind kept wandering to thoughts of Serena. Yes, she certainly is pretty.

He pictured her heart-shaped lips and brown chestnut colored hair that he would like to touch. Suddenly he shook his head, wondering what he was doing thinking about any woman at all, at least, not until he knew her better and talked things over with Nicky.

An hour later Adam strolled down the hall, on the way to his bedroom, he passed Nicky's door and knocked.

"Come in."

"Just wanted to say night," Adam grinned at his daughter. Even though a teenager, she still liked to wear Cinderella pajamas.

Nicky closed her notebook. "Goodnight Dad."

Adam paused before he pulled her door to. "Nicky, how would you feel if I ask someone out on a date?"

Nicky bunched her pillow up and nodded. "I would be okay with it."

"I thought I might ask Ms. Gray out sometime?"

"Dad, you should, she's a nice lady."

"Night Princess." He made way to his room.

After a shower, Adam grabbed his laptop from the side table, slipped under the covers and turned on the bedside light. He booted up his computer and deleted several junk messages, and then clicked the new mail button. He mouthed the words as he typed, "Hi, Serena-it's Adam," in the subject line.

Two weeks had passed since Serena spoke to the class at South Gilman School. She pulled into her driveway, hopped out of the car and with a casual stride moved across the lawn to her front door. Serena's phone buzzed. It took her a few moments to retrieve the cell from her bag. She missed the call, but clicked on the voice mail.

"Hello, Serena, this is Adam."

Adam! Serena quickly unlocked the front door and rushed into the apartment as she listened to Adam's message, "I've enjoyed our emails. I would like to get to know you better. Will you go out to dinner with me?"

Serena instantly hit his number to dial him back.

"Hi, Adam."

"Serena, did you hear my message?"

"Yes." Serena rubbed her forehead, she wanted to go out with him, but a twinge of guilt rose because of the letter and the similar names. She closed her eyes, knowing she should say no, "I would enjoy that."

"Good, I'll pick you up Saturday evening at six."

Serena hung up and mulled over their conversation. She smiled, remembering the pleasant, rich tone of Adam's voice. A piece of a scripture from Psalms 30 came to her mind. "Joy cometh in the morning," but Lord.... Serena's cell rang and interrupted her thoughts. She glanced at Betsy's number.

"Hi, how's the bride to be doing?"

"I've been busy, but I really want to get things done. I have pretty much everything planned out for the wedding so far.... I think." A musical laugh sounded. "So, enough about my wedding tell me what has been going on with you. We haven't talked in several days. Any run ins with men at chicken diners?"

"No, but I'm receiving emails from the Knox family. I get a few from Nicky. Adam and I message each other every day. Nicky asks questions about nursing and writes about stuff at school or her friends. I think she likes talking to me. I find myself turning on my computer just to check my mail.

"Serena that's good, isn't it?"

"It is, but I'm torn over what to do about the letter. I hate keeping information from Adam. I mean I might know he is who Nicky is, who his wife was, and who Nicky's father might really be." She exhaled a fast breath, "Oh, God."

"Serena slow down, take things one day at a time, God will lead you. Have you found anything out for sure?"

"No, I don't know how to approach the subject with him. I only hope I'm listening when the Lord directs me. Until then, I can only trust I'm not making a mistake with what I'm about to do." Her last words came out faster.

"What are you talking about?"

"He called today and asked me to go out to dinner with him."

"Girl, that's great! Go."

"I am. It's odd to be thinking about going on a date with someone again, but I really do want to see him and get to know him better."

"Serena, it's time. Go out with the man and enjoy yourself."

"HERE DAD, LET ME STRAIGHTEN your collar." Nicky adjusted the navy-blue neckline while Adam stood patiently. "Okay. That's better."

"Do you think your old dad will pass Serena's inspection?" He joked even though butterflies were dancing in his stomach.

"Dad, you're not old and you look nice." Nicky laughed. "You're acting like a nervous teenager." Her face took on a serious look.

Adam eyed his daughter with concern. "I know this may be difficult for you. It's the first time I've gone out with anyone since we lost Mom. I can cancel if you are uncomfortable with me going."

"It is hard in a way." She stepped a few feet away. "I can't tell you a lie. It feels weird. I love Mom," Nicky crossed her arms, "but Mom is in heaven, and she would want us to be happy. I guess it's time for you to start seeing someone again, Dad." Adam was quiet for a moment, reflecting on the words his daughter had spoken. "You're right; Mom would want us to be happy." He grabbed his sport jacket. "You know I loved Mom very much, always will, but these past months I've realized I need to make some changes. It's not healthy, us living in the past all the time. Katie will always be in our hearts but we have to go on with lives." Adam watched as his daughter bit on her nail.

"Do you remember what your mom told us right before she passed away?

"Yes, she said she wanted us to live a happy life without her." Nicky looked intently. "Dad, the day before Mom died, she told me that when she was gone, I might discover she kept something from me. She said that she just loved me and wanted me to be happy. I hugged her and she whispered. "Nicky, keep open to possibilities that might come and always remember your dad loves you too. I've wonder what she meant?"

Adam closed the distance between them and wiped a lone tear from his daughter's face. "Mom was in a lot of pain those last few days of her life. The doctors had her on some strong medications. Do you know what that does to people?"

"Yes, Serena told me about Morphine." The young girl shook her head. "It sometimes makes people say things for no reason."

"That's right, but I can tell you one thing, Mom was right about us loving you." Adam closed his arms around his daughter in a hug.

"Dad, you better finish getting ready, you don't want to be late." Nicky reached up and squeezed his shoulders.

As she walked to the hallway, Adam called after her.

"Nicky, you sure you're okay with me going out?"

"It's all right." Nicky paused before she started down the steps. "Even before Mom was on the heavy meds, she told me to encourage you to find another woman to love."

"She did? I can't say anything will happen between Serena and me, but she is a nice lady... and smart."

Nicky giggled, "And you didn't notice she's pretty too?"

The doorbell rang interrupting more conversation. "That's Jan's mom. I'm outta here."

"Don't forget, I'll pick you up at eleven." Adam called out but the sound of the door slamming drowned out his words.

As he drove to Serena's house, the conversation with Nicky played over in Adam's mind. Was Katie talking about the fact that she was pregnant with Nicky when we married? Adam shook his head answering himself. "No." He pictured the conversation they shared when Katie told him that her high school fling never knew she was pregnant and she wanted him to be Nicky's father. Adam turned into the cobblestone drive of Serena's complex. And let out a hard breath. One of the last conversations he had with Katie was difficult because she was feeling guilty for never telling the guy.

The car engine went silent as Adam stared at Serena's Condo. He had to speculate about what would happen if the man whose Nicky's real father showed up. He might want her. I can't lose her too. Adam shook off the uncomfortable thoughts, got out of the car and moseyed to Serena's door.

He knocked and seconds later, she greeted him. "Adam, come in for a minute."

"You have a nice place." He stood waiting for her to gather her handbag.

"I like it. It's spacious."

"I hope you don't mind, but I made reservations at DIGaetti Restaurant."

Serena glanced at her linen pants with the matching pleated jacket, glad she had chosen something appropriate for fine dining. "It sounds wonderful; I haven't had the pleasure of eating there yet."

"I haven't either. My secretary referred to it as casual elegant. Whatever that means." he grinned.

'I'm sure it's a fine place to eat."

They strolled into the restaurant. Adam told the host his name. Serena surveyed the surroundings as they waited for a table. The dining room brought the word stylish culture to Serena's mind.

A large mural theme of the Mediterranean Islands in Sicily dressed the ceiling. At the table, the waiter pulled out Serena's chair. The maître d' took their drink order and handed each a menu.

"This is a nice place." Adam said, taking in the decor.

"Very pretty, I like the dim lighting."

The waiter returned with beverages and bread sticks. They each placed orders for Shrimp and Lobster served over stoned ground Grits with Cheddar Cheese.

"I'm told that is the house specialty." Adam sipped his drink.

"It sounds good and when I heard you mention lobster, I thought I'd try it too."

Adam placed the napkin in his lap. "I know we discussed a lot of things over the internet, but I never ask you when your husband passed away."

"About two years ago, I loved Jason very much. But…" Serena words trailed away and she attempted to grin.

"I know, it's been hard without Katie. I have to be honest; until I met you, I had no desire to be around another woman

again. From the first day we spoke, I wanted to ask you out."

Serena felt her cheeks grow warm. "I know what you mean. I haven't thought about dating either. These past years I've tried to stay positive, but at times it gets me down. I became a home-

body, trying to live in my own little world."

She admired Adam's thick sandy blond hair while they talked. "It's time I made a few changes."

The waiter brought the food and positioned their plates in front of them. When he left, Adam lifted his glass, "to new beginnings, for the both of us."

Serena followed suit, "a new start." She bowed her head and quietly spoke, "thank you Lord, for unexpected possibilities and bless our food. Amen."

Adam raised his head. "I haven't gotten back to that place yet."

"What place?" Serena took a bite of food.

"Leaning on God and trusting Him, I guess. Katie had so much faith, even to the very end. I've spent a lot of time trying to figure out why God let her die."

She sat back. "I know what you mean. I'd be lying if I didn't say that my faith hasn't faltered some in the past couple years, but I've learned one thing being a nurse; Life isn't guaranteed. People are often in the wrong place, like Jason, or they find themselves with sickness. Only God has the answers. We don't understand things now, but one day we will-if we follow the path the Lord sets for us." Serena sipped her beverage. "I do know we all have an eternity to face. It's the Lord, who calls us home, and knowing that... I need to keep my faith strong."

Stillness fell between them. Adam wiped his mouth and stared at Serena. "I never really thought about it like that. I lost my dad many years ago. Mother said God called him home because he was suffering."

"Do you believe that?" Serena scooped up another fork full of shrimp and grits.

"I know the Lord's merciful to his children."

"Well, there's your answer. God is merciful, but we live in a cruel world. The important thing is having a relationship with Jesus Christ. We can't control what happens, but we can determine our destiny."

Adam shook his head. "I never really gave it a lot of thought. All this time I was too busy grieving to think ahead. How did you get so smart?"

Serena snorted. "I'm not smart. After I lost Jason, I kept going to church as much as I could. I try to read the Bible a few times a week. At first, I looked for answers as to why Jason died. I didn't find any exactly, but I found the Lord's comfort. Many nights something in the scriptures would fill my inner being with peace."

Adam gazed at Serena. "So... Am I a lost cause for you?"

A wide grin crossed Serena's face, "No, you're an interesting man. I look forward to getting to know you better." Serena sipped from the crystal goblet. "Have you lived in Greensboro a long time?"

"No. I moved here six years ago, before my wife died." Adam stabbed a shrimp with his fork. "We lived in New Jersey, but we wanted to relocate to a better climate. I searched online for teaching positions and filled out several applications. Then West Gilman emailed, offering me the assistant principal position. It was an offer I couldn't turn down. We relocated to Greensboro. Three years ago, the school board promoted me to principal." Adam took a bite of food and washed it down with his water. "Later, we found out that Katie had cancer."

Serena shallowed hard and it wasn't because of the food. She stared at her diner date who just confirmed that he was from New Jersey. The same place Jason had lived. She wiped her mouth on her napkin and struggled with her words. "I know it must have been hard for you, especially with a daughter."

"Nicky has kept me going."

Serena longed to ask more about Nicky, but only shook her head. "I lived in New Jersey."

Adam's eyes brightened, "Really, where?"

"Jason and I lived in Edison when we first got married and then decided to move to Wilmington."

Adam smiled. "It's a small world. We lived in Millstone, that's about a twenty-minute drive from Edison."

Serena watched Adam and contemplated how she could approach the subject of the letter.

"Nicky is such a lovely young lady. I'll bet you were happy the day she was born."

"Yes, very. Katie and I were young; we couldn't believe how small she was back then. Do you want children someday?" Adam watched Serena her silence was like a thousand words. "I'm sorry I didn't mean to pry or say something out of turn."

Serena raised her hand. "No, it's okay. Jason and I tried to have children, but it never happened."

They lingered over dinner. Adam shared stories of life as a principal of a middle school. Serena highlighted the good things a nurse observes in a daily routine.

At the front of the restaurant Serena waited for Adam to take care of the bill. After paying the check, he strolled to her side and took her hand in his. "I've really enjoyed tonight, Serena."

"Me too," she looked up into his brown eyes and felt her heart beating loudly. They walked hand in hand out to the parking lot.

"Does that mean we can go out again?" Adam unlocked the door, aiming his remote toward the vehicle. He opened her door and waited for Serena to scoot in.

She hesitated to say anything until Adam was in the car.

"Yes, I would like to see you again."

When they pulled in Serena's driveway, Adam walked her to the door.

"I would ask you in, but I know you have a curfew, eleven, is that right?" Serena joked.

They both laughed.

"Yes, I have to pick Nicky up at a friend's house and if I'm late she'll get worried."

"Nicky is such a good girl. I enjoy our talks over the Internet. You're fortunate to have her."

"With her embarking on teen years it's scary." Adam gazed into Serena's eyes. "You're very beautiful." Slowly, he moved closer. He placed his hands on her arms and pulled her close.

His lips touched hers with a gentle kiss.

Serena's heart skipped at the tender caress. For the first time in a long while, she wanted a man to hold her. Serena leaned in to his grasp and allowed him to kiss her a second time.

Adam massaged her lower back, his hands lingered as he kissed her. Finally, he moved away and placed his hands on her shoulders. "I can't wait to see you again."

SERENA'S HAND RESTED on the doorknob as she watched Adam drive away. Once inside the house she peeked out the window toward darkness and then toward the full moon.

With a quick thought, she spun and grabbed her cell phone. Serena knew if Betsy were home, she'd still be awake. After the third ring she answered.

"Am I interrupting anything?"

"Not a thing, girlfriend."

"Didn't you go out with Keith tonight?"

"No. His friend got tickets to the game. They asked me to go, but I really don't like watching sports from those stadium seats. What's up?"

"I just got back from dining with Adam."

"So... Tell me everything."

"It was nice. I like him." Serena reached up and touched her lips. "We kissed goodnight. It felt good to be in his arms. I'm attracted to him."

"Serena, that's great. Did you tell him anything about the letter?"

"No, I couldn't decide how to start the conversation. I could kick myself. I had the perfect opportunity, but listening to him talk about Nicky, I couldn't find the words. It's complicated. Still, if Adam realizes that Nicky is not his biological child, he also needs to know that he is all Nicky has left now."

"Serena, do you think he knows he isn't Nicky's real father?"

Serena walked to the bedroom as they talked. "I don't know if Katie ever told him that he wasn't the father of their child."

"I guess that's something to take into consideration."

"Yeah, I need to find out more before I mention anything that could mess up two people's lives."

Serena yawned. "I'm going to bed. Thinking about all this is giving me a headache. Keep me posted about the details with the wedding. I'll call you later." She hung up the phone, slipped into a comfortable nightgown and climbed into bed. When Serena settled, she lifted a final prayer. "Lord, thank You for bringing Adam and Nicky into my life. Help me to know what and when to tell Adam about Katie's letter."

CHAPTER FOUR

ADAM TOOK SERENA ON a picnic to the lake. He placed a cover on the table and Serena unloaded the basket.

"I wish Nicky could have joined us." Serena sat a bottle of water in front of Adam.

"She would rather go swimming with her friend than hang with us old and boring people."

Serena laughed. "I know. Teenagers, right?" She placed the food in front of Adam and quickly asked a blessing over the food.

Adam repeated, "Amen," and bit into a sandwich. "Do you realize we've being seeing each other for three months?" His eyes held hers as he reached for her hand.

"Yeah, the time has gone by fast."

Adam studied Serena. "I feel like I've known you a long time. I think we make a good couple."

A breeze blew; Serena pushed her hair behind her ear. Her stomach churned a little as it had the last dozen times they dated. "Adam, I need to tell you something. I don't know if you're aware of Nicky's..."

A sound blared out. Adam released her hand and looked at his phone.

"Excuse me, Serena. I need to take Nicky's call."

Serena listened to Adam tell Nicky she couldn't go to a sleep over. Her pleas and offers sounded over the phone and they went back and forth about the reasons. The turmoil of her secret had begun to get the best of her. She hoped it wasn't showing in their relationship.

Adam smiled taking in Serena's grin, and rolled his eyes as he spoke to his daughter. He ended the call and saw Serena frown. "Is everything okay? I'm sorry about the disagreement with Nicky."

"It's fine Adam, I understand." She looked down at the checkered tablecloth. She had been so close to telling him about Nicky being Jason's child before the interruption. Now her nerves were jittery. Her stomach rolled like a tumble weed, tossed by the wind.

Adam reached across the table and held her hand. "You were about to say something about Nicky."

Serena stood and began to pack the basket. "I guess I was going to warn you about the teenage years of a girl."

"I'm sure I'll need pointers. I'll bet you were just as pretty then as you are now."

Serena laughed and folded the table coverlet. "We better go. I heard you agree to take Nicky somewhere in a little while." Adam walked over to Serena. He embraced her in a hug.

"I'm lucky you understand the perils of a single parent."

He picked up the basket and walked beside Serena, to the car.

SERENA WIPED THE MIRROR in the bathroom with her towel before she tossed it over the rack. Serena dried her hair and dressed in easy to remove clothes anticipating the day at the bridal boutique. In the kitchen, she filled her mug with coffee and turned off the pot. After grabbing her suitcase, she headed out the door-ready for a weekend of wedding preparations with her best friend.

BETSY DID A SPIN IN front of Serena.

"That's a lovely dress. You're going to be a beautiful bride. I'm glad you picked the one with the beaded straps.

It's perfect for you."

"Thanks, Serena. I don't mind telling you, I'm nervous.

September isn't that far away."

"You're right, the months will pass quickly, and it'll be a lovely wedding."

"I know. It's just that I want everything perfect. I believe marriage is meant to be once in a life time." Betsy took off the gown and laid it across the chair in the brides' dressing room. For a brief second, she glimpsed Serena's face, expressionless, her eyes downcast to the floor. Betsy slipped into her shift dress and walked a few paces. "Serena, we don't know why things happen, only God does, but I do know the Lord wants His children happy. He has a plan for your life."

Serena's mouth parted with a slight grin. "I know he does, and I'm determined to keep God's will in mind. I'm beginning to have strong feelings for Adam. I just wish things were different."

"In what way?"

Serena brushed her hair and eyed her image in the floor to ceiling mirror. "The letter stands between us. Why do I have to care for Adam? Of all the men I could fall for, it has to be him." She watched her friend gather the veils. "I know the letter came from his Katie and Nicky is really Jason's daughter. She looks so much like him, but how will he feel about it?"

Betsy picked up the wedding accessories and opened the dressing room door.

"You have to tell him and it needs to be done soon."

"I tried the last time we were together. Every time I start to say something, I get a sick feeling. Betsy, this is important. I feel like it could change our relationship."

"It may not. Jason and Katie are gone now." Betsy touched her friend's arm to get her attention. "But it could if he finds out later. Get your courage up and tell the man."

Serena reached for the hanger that held the maid of honor gown. She casually changed the subject. "I like the dark blue one shoulder look, and sash waistline for a bride's maid dress. Come on lady, the fittings are done; our dresses are perfect, now we need to go visit that caterer you spoke about." She turned and walked out of the room.

When the weekend ended, the two women ambled down the sidewalk to Serena's car.

"Serena, I can't believe we got so much accomplished. I ordered the invitations, secured the date for the caterers, got our dresses ordered. Now all I need to do is talk with Keith about the meal for the reception, call the order in, and line up a photographer."

Betsy hugged her friend. "Don't forget to ask Adam and Nicky to the wedding. And pray for the strength to tell him about the letter."

Serena glanced away. "This weekend was fun. You're going to make a beautiful bride. I better go. I want to get back to Greensboro before dark."

SERENA SPENT HER DAY off planting flowers. She had several containers scattered about, some terra cotta pots and one long wooden planter. Serena poured potting soil and planted Wild Petunias, Geraniums and some Hostas. When she finished watering the foliage, she washed her hands, grabbed a soft drink from the refrigerator, and then went back out to the porch.

She pulled the lounger to a canopied spot, where shade covered the area and stretched out in the chair. A light breeze tossed her hair sideways as she contemplated her life in Greensboro. Numerous times, she had attempted to mention the letter to Adam, but each time chocked up. The words to tell him about Katie and her late husband wouldn't come out. Thoughts went to the man who was stealing her heart.

I'm falling in love. I have to do something. I could throw it all away. Maybe I shouldn't mention the letter. "Jesus, I don't want to mess things up." In the warmth, Serena wondered if she had other choices.

The sound of the phone jarred Serena awake. She looked around realizing she had fallen asleep. She swiped at the hair that stuck to her forehead with moisture from the heat.

"Hi, what are you doing on your day off?" A husky voice asked.

"I planted flowers and decorated my patio with some new furniture."

"Sounds like you've been busy." Adam's smooth full-tone voice responded. "Do you still want Nicky and me to come over for dinner later?"

"I do. I hope you don't mind baked chicken and salad."

"It works for me and as long as you add macaroni and cheese. Nicky will be happy. She's not much of a salad eater."

"I'm fixing homemade mac and cheese. It's a recipe my mom used to make."

"You'll spoil her. She only eats it from the box, unless we go out."

Serena laughed. "She deserves to be spoiled. I'll see both of you at six."

"We'll be there. Are we set to go to the theater this weekend?"

"Yes, are you sure Nicky doesn't want to go?"

"No, she has plans. A birthday party and sleep over. Besides, I want you to myself. I missed you last weekend."

"I missed you too, but I had to go to Wilmington and help Betsy with the wedding plans. September is getting close, which reminds me, will you and Nicky accompany me too the wedding? I want you to meet my friend."

"I'd like that. I'll talk to Nicky. Will it be okay with the bride?"

"Yes, she suggested I ask. You'll receive an invitation. September will be here before we know it. Betsy is walking down the aisle on a Saturday evening, and leaving for their honeymoon after the reception. I'll be traveling Friday. I arranged to stay at Betsy's house, until Sunday. She lives in town and there's a nice hotel by her house for you to stay at. Her place is small and only has one bedroom. I'm bunking on the couch."

"Sounds like a plan. I'll ask Nicky, and we'll see you in a few hours."

Serena ended the call, rushed into the kitchen, and pulled out the mixture she'd prepared earlier. She turned on the oven, placing the macaroni and cheese inside. Satisfied that her masterpiece was cooking she went to shower.

"THIS IS GOOD. YOU NEED to teach Dad how to make it." Nicky dished herself out a second helping of the homemade mac and cheese.

"I will, if he wants to learn," She eyed Adam and grinned.

Adam turned his head from one female to the other. "The way Nicky is eating, I don't have a choice."

Nicky giggled, "It's better than the box stuff you make. Serena, Dad says that we're invited to a wedding in Wilmington!"

"Yes, I'd like it very much if both of you would go with me. My best friend is getting married"

"I don't have anything to wear to a fancy event." Nicky washed her food down with a drink of iced tea.

"Hum... That is a dilemma. We could go to the mall in a couple of weeks, make it a day out with breakfast, dress shopping and I can teach you how to make my famous mac and cheese."

"Dad, can I go?" Nicky faced Adam excitedly.

"Sure. Serena's probably better at dress shopping than I am."

"Probably!" Nicky tossed her head back. A silly laugh filled the kitchen.

As the night ended, Serena stood on the porch with Adam "This was a good evening." He held her hand and squeezed it gently. I wish I could kiss you passionately."

"Dad, let's go! Nicky stuck her head out of the car window and yelled."

"You better take her home, Adam." Serena wet her lips, longing to feel his mouth on hers.

"When you and Nicky go shopping next week, I will fire up the grill? We'll cook out. I'm a fair outdoor chef, if I do say so myself." He lifted her hand to his lips and kissed her fingers.

"I can't wait to taste your creations." Serena smiled and placed a kiss on his cheek.

Adam returned the caress and tuned to walk to the car while Serena watched them leave.

THE PEDIATRIC WING was quiet. Serena stepped into the nurse's break room and turned on her phone to see a missed call from Betsy. While she fed coins into the snack machine, she called her friend.

"Are you okay? Your message sounded alarming. All you said was call me."

"I'm fine now. I just panicked. The wedding photographer cancelled."

"Oh no, what are you going to do?" She seated herself at a table and opened a bag of chips.

"It's worked out. Keith went to school with someone who is a professional photographer. He's going to take pictures at the wedding for free if I let him use some of the snapshots in his portfolio. How is everything with you?"

"Going well, I asked Adam if he and Nicky wanted to come to the wedding. He said yes."

"Good I can't wait to meet the man who's stolen your heart."

"Did I say that?" Serena munched on another chip.

"Not in so many words, but we've been friends long enough, I see the signs." A chuckle met Serena's ear.

"Betsy, I may not say anything about the letter, so mum's the word"

"Not tell him. Is that wise?"

"I don't know, but I'm afraid of his reaction. It's weird, having a letter from his dead wife and then we meet and start dating. Not to mention the little boy at the hospital and what he said. Would Adam believe that? He might think that I had purposely tried to meet him, planned to ruin his life with the information..."

"Serena, sometimes things happen we can't explain. You don't know why. Maybe Adam needs to know the truth for closure."

After they hung up, Serena sat gazing out the window wishing that she had the answer.

THE WEEK FLEW BY FOR Serena. Several times throughout her rounds at the hospital, she caught herself humming.

Today, she clocked her time and headed to the elevator, two days of rest before her. As she strolled to her car, she eyed the trees and caught sight of a few roses peeping out for the sunshine. "Lord, I'm so glad I made this move." She started the car and pulled out onto the main road with a couple days off in front of her. I won't be resting tomorrow. Nicky and I are going shopping.

SERENA RANG THE BELL. Adam swung open the front door and pulled her into his arms, their lips met. She stepped away and stared into his eyes, her heart fluttered as they kissed again. Before she could say anything, the door swung open wider and a voice blared.

"Let's go. I'm ready."

Adam raised an eyebrow and eyed his daughter. "Nicky, let Serena catch her breath before you hurry her away."

"Dad, we have a lot of girl stuff to do."

He grinned at his daughter and turned his attention to Serena. "Well, I guess I'll see you two this evening. Call me when you get ready to bring her home and I'll start the grill."

"OUT OF ALL THE DRESSES I've tried on this one is the best." Nicky stepped from the dressing room. She twirled around examining the purple twist top party dress with the high-low hemline. "I like the way the hem lays above my knees in the front, and goes long in back."

"It is pretty, and the square neckline is lovely on you. Let's pay for it and go to the Shoe Palace, you need heels to complete the outfit. Then we'll head to my house and I'll teach you to make homemade mac and cheese."

Serena drove to the shoe store. Nicky took another hour finding the perfect pair of shoes to complement her dress. Serena also picked out a new pair for herself. She paid for her athletic wear and grinned at Nicky handing the sales clerk her dad's credit card.

THEY WENT BACK TO SERENA'S place and stood in the kitchen preparing to cook.

"Hold this." Nicky slid a ring on Serena's third finger and watched it barely pass the knuckle.

"Okay, but why did you take it off?"

"To wash my hands, it's not real, just costume jewelry. My friend and I have one alike."

Serena glimpsed the half-moon shaped ring with jagged edges and then grinned, "Oh, I see. It's a friendship ring."

"Yeah, Jan has the rest of the letters on hers. You can lay it over there if you want." She motioned to the table.

Nicky cracked eggs in a bowl while Serena set the cheddar Cheese out on the counter.

"This is easier than I thought it would be." Nicky drained the macaroni.

"Yes, it's a simple recipe. We'll take it to your house. Adam can sample your dish."

"He'll be surprised. Dad is used to me opening up boxes or taking stuff out of the freezer when I cook." Nicky reached for the Paprika. "Serena, I know you and Dad have been dating a few months. Can I ask you a question?"

Serena placed a casserole dish on the cupboard. "Sure, you can ask me anything."

"Do you like my dad? I mean really like him." Not waiting for an answer, she rushed the rest of her words. "I loved Mom, but sometimes I miss not having a woman in the house. Dad's great, but he doesn't know anything about girl stuff."

"Nicky, I like spending time with you too and I know how you feel about your mom. My husband passed away. It's hard losing someone you love." Serena let out a slow breath. "I don't know what the future holds for your dad and me, but I do care a great deal for him. Matter-of-fact, Adam is the first man I've wanted to be around since Jason died. She turned on the stove. "Now, let's get these ingredients mixed and, in the oven, so we can show your dad that lovely dress you found."

As Serena watched Nicky work in the kitchen, she contemplated saying something, maybe probing to see if Nicky knew anything about Katie and Jason. "Nicky about your mom..."

Nicky's phone sounded and she grabbed it and started chatting to her friend. Minutes later, Nicky stuck the cell back in her jean pocket. "Serena I'm sorry, what were you going to say about Mom?"

"Nothing, except that I'm sure she loved you very much."

CHAPTER FIVE

SERENA PULLED INTO the Knox family's circle drive. Nicky grabbed her bags from the back seat and headed to the house.

"Dad!" Nicky yelled as she opened the door.

Adam crossed through the kitchen from the back deck and went into the living room. "You sound happy. He smiled at his daughter. "I have the steaks almost done. Are you ladies ready to eat?" He walked over to Serena and kissed her on the cheek.

She handed him a covered dish. "This is Nicky's homemade macaroni and cheese."

"Really, you got her to cook!" Adam eyed his daughter.

"I cook. Some." She reached inside the bag and pulled out the new outfit. "Isn't it beautiful?"

"It's a great dress, Nicky. I'm glad Serena was able to take you shopping. I'm still recovering for our last outing at the mall." Adam tasseled his daughter's hair.

"Dad, don't mess my hair up. Besides, it wasn't that bad. You just need to loosen up." Nicky grabbed her shoes and jogged up the stairs to her room.

"Don't be too long, it's time to eat." He looked in the direction his daughter hurried. "The mall excursion wasn't unpleasant for her, but my little girl is growing up. Shopping with a teenage, that's a challenge."

Serena chuckled and glanced towards the staircase. "She's blessed to have you as her father."

"Come on," He reached for Serena's hand and led her out to the patio.

Adam placed the steaks on plates and took them to the sunroom. Serena poured tea into their glasses.

Nicky came in with her homemade favorite and placed the dish on the table. "I really did make this. Serena only told me what ingredients to add," she announced as everyone took a seat.

"She's a natural in the kitchen." Serena reached out, took Nicky's hand, and then bowed her head. Adam glanced at his daughter, who also had her head bowed. He paused a second before closing his eyes to the sound of prayer.

With the final Amen, Adam scooped out a serving from the casserole dish.

"I know it's going to be good."

The three of them enjoyed their meal. Nicky chatted about the shopping trip. After dinner, Nicky and Serena cleared the table, while Adam cleaned the grill.

"I'll load the dishwasher you sit in the swing with Dad." Nicky pointed towards the sun porch.

"Okay, but yell if you need help."

Nicky stacked plates and then stepped out to the deck where Adam and Serena sat. "Dad, I'm going to my room. I'll see you in the morning."

Adam hugged her and then Nicky enfolded Serena in her arms before heading back inside.

"I enjoyed our shopping trip."

Serena returned Nicky's hug. "I had fun too; we'll do it again sometime."

Adam and Serena rocked in slow motion. He scooted close and put his arm around her shoulders.

"Nicky's a sweet young lady." She slid into Adams embrace. "Yes, she is. After Katie's death, she had a rough time. Her grades fell and she started sneaking out at night. I don't mind telling you, for a while I didn't know what to do."

"She seems fine now." Serena noted the stars starting to peek out.

"I'm thankful for that. I just kept talking to her, reminding her of things her mom would expect, and assuring her that

Katie would be proud of her. Slowly things started to change."

She rested her head on Adam's shoulder. When there was a lull in the conversation, Serena's mind wandered to Betsy's conversation.

"Adam did you and Katie get married at a young age?"

"Yes, we did. Katie had just graduated from high school and I was in my second year of college. She was my roommate's sister. I fell in love with her the first time I saw her. Why do you ask?"

Serena straightened and swallowed a lump in her throat.

"I'm only curious. I guess you two wanted a family right off."

"I never really thought about the timing. Nicky was born the first year of marriage. I never regretted having a family."

She looked sideways at Adam and saw his jaw muscles wiggle as he stared out into the night. She placed her hand on Adam's arm. An idea she'd pondered on earlier, came forth.

Adam, will you and Nicky go with me to the morning worship service?"

Adam didn't answer. The silence lingered. After what seemed like eternity, he cleared his throat. "I've been thinking about the things you said about faith. It's made me realize I've slipped back into some worldly ways." He put his arm over Serena's shoulder and kissed her. "It's time for me to renew my faith. Nicky and I need to get back to church."

"Why don't you two pick me up in the morning? Salvation's Door isn't far from my house and it's a good worship center."

"I know that church, it's the brick one on the corner of Elm Street."

"Yeah, that's the one. I've been attending since I moved here, when my schedule allows." She rose from the seat. "I hate to end the evening, but I'd better go."

Adam walked Serena to the living room. For the first time, Serena paid attention to the furnishings. "I like this burgundy leather living room set."

"Thanks. Nicky picked it out. A year ago, I decided to get new furniture. I figured Nicky would enjoy helping me make the decision about decorating and honestly, we both needed to change the looks of this space." Adam grinned and pointed to a Hunter Green recliner, "except for that. I couldn't get rid of my favorite sleeping chair."

Serena chuckled at his remark while she scanned the other side of the room. She noticed a photo sitting on the bookcase in the corner. Serena took a few steps to the shelf and surveyed the picture. A woman with long hair and a huge smile sat between Adam and Nicky. "Is this Katie?"

"Yes, that photograph was taken before her diagnosis. Right after that she started Radiation and Chemotherapy." He shook his head. "She lost all of her beautiful hair."

"I'm sorry your family had to go through such a weakening disease." Serena rested her hand on his arm and then walked toward the front door. "As a nurse I see too much suffering."

"I suppose you do. Katie was a special woman. In the year she suffered, she never stopped having faith. I think back to some conversations we had in those last months. Katie hung on to the hope of a healing, but commented that she was staying true to the Lord, because if it was her time to go home to Heaven, she planned to be ready." Adam closed the distance between them.

"It sounds like she was a strong and true woman of faith."

Adam nodded and took hold of Serena's hand. "She made me promise I would stay close to the Lord and find someone else to love. Until now, I didn't realize I wasn't keeping my promises very well. Before you came along the thought of sharing my life with someone else was hard to imagine."

Adam's hand went to the back of Serena's neck. He played with her hair as he leaned close. She welcomed the caress, which quickly turned from one lingering kiss to another.

She sighed, as Adam's soft, smooth lips met hers. Even though she wanted to stay in his arms she but pulled back. When their eyes met, she saw the same passion on Adam's face as she felt inside. "I'd better go. I'll see you in the morning," her words unsteady.

NICKY, SAT IN THE BACKSEAT, tapped on Serena's shoulder to get her attention, and began questioning her about the upcoming wedding. Adam took a sideways glance at Serena while she responded to his daughter's inquiries. The chatter of their voices filled the car.

"We're here." Adam pulled into the parking lot of the worship center.

"Dad, it's been years since we've been to church."

"Too long, Nicky we're going to get back to the routine of attending church on Sundays. The Lord has provided blessings and we need to be the Christians we once were."

The light shone through a stained-glass window as Nicky and Adam followed Serena to a pew six aisles away.

"Carole, this is Adam Knox and his daughter Nicky." Serena pointed to her guest.

"It's nice to meet you both." Carole tilted her head and smiled up at Adam, and then reached out and clasped Nicky's hand. "I'm glad you came. We have a wonderful youth class. I think you'll enjoy it."

The orator began the service. Serena and Adam listened to a choir sing "Amazing Grace," then they stood to join in with a hymn. Serena glanced at Adam. Her ears caught the sound of his bass voice singing out "Knell at the Cross," while they followed along with the words on the overhead projector.

The minister spoke on trusting the Lord. Serena and Adam flipped the pages in their Bibles while he directed the congregation to turn to Psalms 118:8. Pastor Bob stepped in front of the podium and put emphasis on the first part of the scripture.

"It is better to trust in the Lord," he commented and then stepped back behind the podium and verbally listed ways to apply faith to everyday life. Turn to Proverbs, 3:5-6." He continued to preach on having confidence in God. Serena felt Adam's hand enclose hers while they listened to the morning message.

After service, Adam and Serena spoke to people in the back of the sanctuary while waiting for Nicky to join them. Adam stood beside Serena and gave a friendly, "hello," when she introduced him.

"I enjoyed the service." Adam grinned at Serena. "At times I thought he was preaching only to me."

Serena agreed. "Isn't it usually like that? Whenever there was a really good message my mother used to say, He's stepping on my toes"

"You're right. I think I moved my feet back under the seat a little, toward the end of his message." He looked ahead as a crowd of teens made their way into the sanctuary. "There's my girl." Adam slung his arm on Nicky's shoulder as she joined them. "Are you lovely ladies ready for lunch?"

They nodded in agreement and walked to the lobby.

"Dad, I like this church. I got to sit next to one my classmates from school."

On the way out, Pastor Bob greeted them. "Serena it's good to see you today."

"Thanks, this is Adam Knox and his daughter, Nicky."

The head of the church shook hands with Adam. "It's good to have you and your daughter. I do hope you'll join us again."

"Thank you, Pastor, we may do that. We need to get back into church." Adam glanced away at his omission of not attending services.

"Call me Pastor Bob, everyone does, and Adam I'm a phone call away if you need anything. I look forward to seeing you and Nicky next Sunday."

THE RESTAURANT WAS crowded. Noise of chatter filled the room. As the host escorted them to a table beside a large window, Serena took a quick look at the huge fish aquarium. Her eyes tagged the tank with a big orange and white clown fish as they seated themselves.

"I like fish. You know I may buy some. I have the perfect place to set up an aquarium."

"Serena, can I help you pick out some fish?" Nicky glanced at the fish tank while she spoke.

"Sure, you can. I may even ask your dad to help me take them home." She smiled at Adam.

"I'm game, when do we shop for these fish?"

The waitress took each person's order, everyone but Nicky ordered flounder.

"How come you didn't get fish? I know you like shrimp."

Adam raised his eyebrow at his daughter.

"I do and I also enjoy crab, but I can't eat fish while Serena talks about buying some for pets."

Serena laughed. "I can, except I won't eat the cute tropical ones. So, are we up for a shopping trip after lunch? There's a pet store a few blocks from here."

Everyone agreed as the server placed the plates with mouth-watering seafood before them and one piled with spaghetti in front of Nicky.

Adam glanced around the table. "I don't mind helping you get a fish tank organized." He reached for his daughter's hand, and she took hold of Serena's. "Lord, thank you for this meal.

Bless the food and the times we are together."

"Okay everyone eat-up, we're going shopping." Nicky scooped a fork full of noodles.

THE THREE OF THEM STROLLED down the aisles of Pet-A-Rama. Serena and Adam stopped in front of a long line of fish tanks.

Nicky kept walking and raised her voice a little.

"Dad I'm going over here and look at these kittens."

"This is what I want some Clown fish." Serena pointed to a tank.

A young man approached them. "May I help you find something?"

"Yes, I want an aquarium, with a few fish. I like vivid colors, like the clown fish."

The clerk scratched his head. "Well, if you have Clown fish, you'll need a saltwater tank. Those species are different from others. They require more care."

"No. I don't think I want that. I need something easy to maintain."

"Then you want to get some of these fish." He motioned to the tank next to Serena. "These are fresh water. What size aquarium do you want?"

Serena looked toward the end on the passageway at the tanks displayed. "I want one that size." She pointed to a twenty-gallon container.

"Okay, that's a good household size. I wouldn't recommend getting any more than ten fish."

Serena examined the fish. "I don't want ten fish, maybe five of six." She looked at Adam who was standing by listening.

"Adam, what do you think?"

Adam gazed at the fish. "I think six is a good number. I like that Goldfish." His finger trailed after a bright orange fish that looked like it had eaten too much.

Serena's face lit with joy. "He's fat!"

"He has character." In the background, they heard Nicky calling to Adam. "I better go and see what Nicky's doing. I'll leave the choices to you. I'm just along to help you get the fish home and their house set-up."

Adam walked to the other side of the store, and Serena stared in the big tank. "I guess the first one is going to be that huge Goldfish."

"Dad, come on, can I have him?" Nicky held a Siamese kitten close.

"Who is going to take care of that cat?" Adam watched as his daughter cuddled the kitten.

"I will. I promise. He's so... cute. We can put the litter box in the laundry room. Then when I wash clothes, I'll remember to change it for Baxter."

"Baxter?" Adam shook his head and laughed. "I guess if you already named the cat, we'll have to take him home." Adam looked at his daughter, a serious tone in his voice. "You have to promise me that you'll tend to him, which means feed him every day and keep a clean litter box."

Adam watched Nicky reach for her pet. She snuggled it closer, while her eyes sparkled from happiness. "I will Dad."

An hour later, they walked out of the store. Adam carried the tank, filled with all the necessities to board fish. Serena held a shopping bag with a Goldfish, three Tetras, one orange and blue and two red and sapphire. She'd also purchased two Zebra Danios. Nicky trailed behind with Baxter in a cardboard box and other supplies.

NICKY SAT ON THE END of the couch playing with Baxter, Serena and Adam placed the gravel and ornaments in the aquarium.

"I'm glad we stopped and picked up twenty gallons of water."

"Yeah, I bet the cashier wondered what it was for."

Behind them Nicky added, "You guys made me tote most of it in!"

Adam laughed at his daughter, "Consider that pay for Baxter."

"Baxter I'll take good care of you." She nudged his face.

Serena looked at Nicky and then Adam. They both smiled at the show of affection Nicky gave the kitten. As the evening drew near night, Nicky hugged Serena goodbye.

"Nicky, will you take Baxter to the car. I'll be right there." Adam watched as she grabbed the box with her kitten and head to the vehicle.

"Serena, I've had a good day." He embraced her and trailed kisses from her neck to mouth, before he moved back and then traced the outline of her mouth with his thumb.

Serena drew in a shaky breath. "I enjoyed today a lot."

"I need to get Nicky home. Serena, you've become very important to me. I count each day until I can see you again."

Adam ran his finger over her cheek.

"You're also a big part of my life. And of course, I think Nicky is wonderful."

"I'm glad you said that. After all the talk the other night, I was afraid you were second guessing a relationship with a man and his teenage daughter. I'd be disappointed if you were. I want the woman I'm serious about to also love my daughter and I can see you do."

"Adam, never think that I don't. I do care about you and Nicky." Serena ran her hand across his chest.

Adam pulled her closer and kissed her. When he released her, he grabbed Serena's hand and held it to him.

"Let's go out Friday, just the two of us. I'll pick you up at six. We can have a meal somewhere and maybe go to a movie."

"I'll be ready." She smiled and walked with him to the front door.

She listened to the car back out of the driveway and walked over to the fish tank. Serena flipped on the hood light. Her eyes followed the big Goldfish. "Well Adam, I hope you like your new home." She chuckled at the name she had given the fish.

SERENA MADE HER ROUNDS at the hospital. Lunchtime came and she went to the cafeteria and purchased her meal. Strolling through the room, she searched for a seat.

"Serena, join me." Carole stopped chewing and motioned to the empty chair.

"Thanks." Serena set her tray down and scooted in the chair. She bowed her head and quietly asked a blessing.

"The man I met at church, is that your boyfriend?"

Serena reached for her sandwich and grinned at her friend's words. "I guess you can say that. He is the principal at the school where I went on career day. We started talking and we've been going out ever since."

"He's very good-looking and seems like a nice man."

"Adam is wonderful. His daughter is sweet too."

"Is he divorced?" Carole scooped up a spoonful of vegetables.

"No, his wife died about the same time my husband passed away."

"Oh my, unfortunately that's something you have in common."

"Yes, but we have other mutual interest."

Carole swallowed the last bite of her food. "You two make a good couple."

The women discussed the afternoon work schedule and exchanged pleasantries about cooking and hairstyles. Serena watched Carole glance at her watch.

"Oh dear, I'm running behind. I'll see you later."

ON FRIDAY EVENING, Serena took one last glance in the bathroom mirror before she answered the doorbell. "Come in."

Adam walked across the threshold, kissed Serena and spotted the tank. "I see the fish seem to be happy."

"Yes, everything is fine. And Adam is getting bigger." She turned to get her pocketbook from its resting place on the chair.

"I beg your pardon." Adam looked in her direction and lifted his eyebrow.

Serena laughed. "That big Goldfish, I named him Adam." He grinned at the fish, then Serena. "I don't know if I should be flattered or start thinking about a serious diet plan."

"No silly. You're perfect, but you liked that fish so he had to be your namesake."

Adam enclosed her in an embrace and kissed her again. Her soft body against his gave way to thoughts about how life would be with her in his arms all the time.

THEY WENT TO AN ITALIAN restaurant and then to the theater to watch a new release. In the dark, Adam rested his arm on her shoulder and chuckled at the romantic comedy. After the film ended, they strolled casually to the car.

Adam opened the door for Serena and waited for her to get inside. "The movie was better than I thought it would be for a comedy."

"Yes, it was pretty good. Would you have rather watched that film about the mob?"

"No, I liked that show."

Adam pulled into Serena's driveway. He walked her to the door and waited for her to unlock the apartment, "If you don't have to go yet, we could sit on the glider a while?"

"I like that idea." His eyes lit up. "Nicky's spending the night at her friend's house." In a grand movement, he bowed and waved his hand in the direction of the back deck, "lead the way madam."

A full moon shown, Serena leaned against Adams shoulder and gazed at the stars. For the longest time she was still. "What's on your mind?" Adam hugged her closer.

"Hum... nothing really. I'm just enjoying the evening." Serena answered.

Adam kissed the top of her head. "Serena, there's something I need to tell you," His smooth voice sounded solemn.

Serena moved out of his embrace and looked at his face silently questioning the quick change in the tone of his voice.

"Okay, what is it?"

"I'm falling in love with you." Adam gently squeezed her palm and rushed out the words.

She could tell the way he stopped talking and eyed her that he was waiting for her to make a comment. Serena thought about it. Her soul wanted to scream out that she loved him too, but her mind questioned the feelings. The secret she held from him was like sandpaper, which grinded away to make her feel as if she was hurting their relationship.

A Bible verse from the Song of Solomon came to her remembrance. "Let him kiss me with the kisses of his mouth: for thy love is better than wine." She pushed back her hair. "Adam, I can't imagine you not being in my life now. You've made me realize I can love again."

CHAPTER SIX

SERENA WAS BUSY AT the hospital but when she wasn't working, she spent as much time as possible with Adam. Numerous times she tried to tell him about the letter. It seemed with each chance she had an interruption made her chicken out.

After a long day at the hospital, she returned home and took off her shoes. Serena leaned back on the couch, sipping on a cola. She focused on the aquarium, relaxing while watching fish swim from one end to another. The bright orange goldfish suspended itself close to the front of the tank and captured her attention. Serena grinned at its lips wiggling. The phone buzzed and broke the gaze she and the fish shared.

"Betsy, how are things?"

"Stressful, but in a good way."

"Well, you don't have long."

"I know. I can't believe in a week I'll be a married woman."

Serena smiled as she listened to her friend's enthusiastic comments. "I'm happy for you. Is everything ready for the big day?"

"Yes, Keith is like that fast food commercial. He has me checking and double-checking all the arrangements. Tell me, how things are going with you and Adam?"

"It's wonderful." Serena put her feet up on the coffee table.

"I feel a little guilty."

"Why?"

"I still haven't said anything about the letter. I'm not sure
Adam knows anything about Nicky's conception. Maybe,
he believes she is his child. Betsy, I love Adam and don't want
to hurt him."

"Serena, that's great, but you know you have to tell him."

"I don't know. Every time I start to say something, I can't
find the words. Then I lose courage. I've decided to throw the
letter away and forget I ever saw it."

"Are you sure you can do that?"

"It's what I need to do." Serena shook her head, even
though Betsy couldn't see her. "I love Nicky too and won't risk
messing up their lives."

"Well," Betsy voice sounded doubtful. "You have to do
what feels right, but pray about this situation."

"I will." Serena heard a beep through the phone.

"That's Keith telling me he's in the driveway. He coming to
dinner so we can go over the detail and make sure all is ready.

I'll see you in a few days."

"Okay. I'm picking up Adam and Nicky, and we'll be there
Friday evening."

THE SUITCASES WERE in the car. They had traveled I-40
for three hours.

"Is there a place I can rent a car once we're there?"

Serena glanced to her right. "Why would you want to rent
a vehicle?"

"To get back to the motel, I know you'll want to spend time with Betsy."

"Yes, we have an appointment in the morning to get our hair done, but you don't need to rent a car. You can drive mine. I'll use Betsy's if I need too."

They veered off the Interstate to the Wilmington exit. A few miles later, passed a church and Serena motioned to the white building. "That's the worship center Betsy's getting married at." She drove a block, and then turned the corner. They passed Jackson Hotel. Serena nodded toward the tall building.

"I thought you and Nicky might like to stay there."

"It's fine by me, how about it, Nicky?"

Nicky leaned toward the window. "Sure, it'll work. I'm not picky."

A block later Serena pulled in the driveway of a cottage style house. "We're here, this is where Betsy lives."

The front door flung open and Betsy met them halfway. Serena hugged her friend then turned back to Adam and Nicky.

"Betsy, I want you to meet Adam and Nicky Knox."

"It's good to meet both of you. I've heard a lot about you."

"I hope it was all good." Adam reached out and shook Betsy's hand.

"Only nice things I assure you." See turned to Nicky.

"You're a very pretty young lady." "Thank you." Nicky smiled.

Serena sighed with relief. She wasn't sure if Adam and Nicky would like Betsy, or if Betsy would like them. So far, it seemed that they would all get along just fine.

Betsy turned and began to walk towards the house. "Let's go inside. I have sandwiches."

Adam clapped his hands together. "I can always eat. That is, if I'm not too fat for you Serena?"

Serena laughed at Adam's noticed Betsy's confused look. "I named my goldfish Adam. But the fish is fat, so Adam thinks he is fat."

Betsy smiled and led them to her Galley Kitchen. Like a food line in a cafeteria, each made their way to the paper plates, bottled water, and sandwich slices with potato chips. In the dining room, they took a seat at the square table. Everyone's head bowed as Betsy thanked the Lord for the food.

After they ate, Adam called the motel and secured adjoining rooms for him and Nicky. He stretched his legs out in the chair as Nicky slipped her shoes off and curled her feet up reading a teen magazine while the grown-ups talked about the coming ceremony.

As they talked about wedding plans and discussed the trip from Greensboro to Wilmington, Adam noticed Nicky yawn with sleepy eyes.

"I think Nicky and I will go to the hotel." He slid to the edge of the seat.

"Do you know how to get to the church tomorrow evening?" Betsy stood.

"Yes, Serena took us by on the way here. It's only a mile down this road."

"Good, I'll see you two at the church then. I'm so happy you could come."

Adam smile at Betsy. "I'm glad you invited us."

"Betsy, I'm going to walk them to the car." Serena headed to the door.

The stars flickered in the sky and a street light cast a shadow across the yard. Adam reached for Serena's hand as they walked slowly to the driveway. Adam took the keys, Serena offered.

"You sure you're fine with us using your car."

"It's the easiest way. I'll be riding with Betsy." She reached over to Nicky and hugged her. "I hope both of you can find something to do tomorrow. I'm afraid my schedule is full. Betsy and I have several appointments. We need to make sure the church is decorated, the right flowers arrive on time, and the caterers don't have any last-minute problems. Betsy also wants

to go over everything with the photographer."

Adam grinned as Serena listed the things they'd be doing.

"I didn't realize so much has to be done for a one-day event."

"Dad, a woman has to do these things if she wants a nice wedding." Nicky rolled her eyes at her father's ignorance.

Adam shook his head and looked at both of them. "I know what I'm up against, when this one gets married." He leaned over and gave Nicky a hug.

"Yes, and she will make a beautiful bride." Serena eyes lit with assurance.

"Why don't you get in the car I'll be there in a minute?" Adam watched Nicky nod and seat herself in the passenger's side of the vehicle.

"Are you sure you won't get bored until time for the wedding?"

"No. Nicky and I are going to Carolina Beach for a few hours." Adam leaned closer to Serena and kissed her.

She opened her eyes as he stepped away. "Be sure to have breakfast at that Greek restaurant next to the boat docks, the food is wonderful. I'll see you both around four."

"Will do." Adam and Nicky drove off. Serena turned and made her way back into Betsy's house. She found Betsy cleaning the table off.

Betsy's mouth widened with a grin. "So, that's Adam? He is handsome."

"Yes, he is." Serena absentmindedly tossed an empty bottle away.

"Okay, so he's nice looking and smart. What's the problem?"

"You know." Serena placed condiments in the refrigerator. "I just wish things weren't complicated?"

Betsy gazed at her friend. "Serena, sometimes we make things difficult by our choices. There is no answer, except the one you're comfortable with. Pray that God leads you in this situation. The longer a problem lingers the harder it is to fix."

Serena shook her head, "I know you're right. If I tell him about the letter will I lose the man I love?"

Betsy wiped the table off as Serena talked. "If you don't tell him, can you live with it?"

"I don't know. I'm going to lie down. I'll see you in the morning." Serena walked into the other room. She made the couch up with a pillow and blanket. As she laid in the dark room, his mind traveled the road of possibilities that her secret could create.

THE WOMEN SAT SIDE by side. Each had a beautician styling their hair. "I'm so glad we could do this. I miss going to the beauty salon together."

"I do too. I don't do near enough shopping without you around," laughter floated in the room.

Betsy stared at Serena. "Seriously, I'm glad you are happy, and it's wonderful you have Adam in your life. Have you ever thought that all this was meant to be?"

Serena frowned at her friend in confusion. "What do you mean?

"Your moving, and finding Adam the way you did. Serena, I think God guided you to him." Betsy closed her eyes as the hairdresser pinned some hair up. "The man obviously adores you, and Nicky thinks the world of you, I can tell."

"I know and I love both of them so much. That's why I'm afraid if I reveal the contents of the letter to Adam, and he doesn't know he's not Nicky's biological father, I'll hurt a wonderful family."

They both sat silently for a few minutes. The hairdresser styling their hair finished with Betsy and removed the covering. She stood and admired her hair piled high in the back. "I don't know, Serena. I wish I did." Betsy thanked the stylist. "I'll pay and meet you at the front entrance."

Five minutes later Serena joined Betsy at the counter. They admired one another's hair styles then stepped outside and strolled down the sidewalk to the car. Serena looked intently at her friend. "Betsy, you have to promise me you'll never speak of that letter to anyone, not even Keith. I suppose this has to be a secret we'll take to our graves."

Betsy frowned. "You're serious?" After seconds of silence, she replied. "Okay, you're my best friend. If you want me to keep quiet, I will."

Serena smiled at Betsy. "Thanks, it's the only answer I have right now. What's next on our agenda?"

"How about lunch and then we'll go to the church and see how the decorations look. I need to call the caterers. I forgot to tell them to park the van behind the community center to unload for the reception."

AN HOUR BEFORE THE wedding the women stood in the nursery, the room connected to a large private powder room where Betsy chose to change into her wedding attire. Serena gazed at her friend's bridal gown. Beads lined the straps running the length of the v-neckline. The front of the gown touched her toes and the back fanned out like a train. "Betsy, you look beautiful. I'm glad you choose to have your hair styled with matching beads instead of a veil."

"Betsy admired the dress in the floor to ceiling mirror. "I was worried I'd be nervous. I figured a covering over my face would only make things worse."

Serena hugged her. "I'm going to the corridor. Remember, listen for the processional music, and then walk into the hallway." She grinned and gave a small wave as she stepped out of the room.

Serena stood in the lobby as Keith approached from the front of the church. "Is my bride ready?"

"She is. You look nice and Betsy is beautiful. I'm happy for both of you."

"I knew she would make a lovely bride. I'm glad the wedding is finally here. All I want is to start married life with the woman I love." Keith adjusted his bow tie.

Serena caught sight of Adam and Nicky and motioned for them to come over. "Keith, I want you to meet Adam Knox and Nicky, his daughter."

The men shook hands and Keith bowed his head and smiled a wide toothy grin at Nicky.

"I'm glad you came. Adam, maybe when Betsy and I get back from our honeymoon, and settle in, we can all get together and watch a game or something."

"That works for me." Adam and Keith continued to talk.

The whole time Adam kept turning his eyes to Serena.

The music changed and Keith jerked his head toward the piano. "That's my cue. I'd better get the best man and find my place beside the minister." Keith moved down the hall to the main part of the worship center.

"Serena you're beautiful." Adam's eyes followed her dress from the floor to her neckline.

"I like your hair with ringlets hanging down." Nicky reached out and touched a curl on Serena' cheek.

"Thank you, Nicky, you look wonderful too. Did your dad help you with your hair?"

Nicky put her hand on her mouth to stifle a laugh. "Are you serious? Dad can't braid hair. There is a beauty shop in the hotel. They fixed it."

Adam pressed his lips together to keep from smiling. "We better sit down the wedding is about to begin. Serena, I'll see you at the reception." he kissed her cheek and took Nicky's hand to find their seat.

The bridal march began. Serena paced slowly down the aisle. Betsy walked to the front and took her place beside Keith. The minister started the ceremony. Serena paid attention to every detail. It had been a long time since she'd attended a wedding and the words of the ceremony struck her. "Till death do you part." Lord I hear you. Jason and I had a good life.

Adam sat beside Nicky and watched the service as he listened to a Bible verse.

"'Whoso findeth a wife findeth a good thing, and obtaineth favour of the Lord,' the verse, ladies and gentlemen is from Proverbs 18:22."

The minister announced the couple as man and wife and concluded the ceremony.

The words, findeth a wife spun around in Adam's mind.

"Have I found a good thing Lord?"

PAPIER MACHE BELLS and balloons hung from the ceiling. Tables extended almost the entire length of a wall with a selection of finger foods. There were various flavors of bread sticks, deli trays, cheeses, chicken wings, and shrimp cocktails. The last table held a variety of sweets, fruit parfaits, a fondue station, and assorted beverages. A setting by itself displayed a chocolate wedding cake with butter cream icing; small colored florets adorned the top and sides.

Serena searched pass the round tables scatted in the room, until she spotted Nicky.

"There you are!"

"Isn't this magnificent, if I get married, I want a ceremony just like this someday." Nicky's eyes scanned the decorations.

Overhearing Nicky, Adam walked closer.

"I better start putting more money in the saving account if this is what I'm facing."

"Dad I'm going over to the fondue table." Nicky glanced in his direction and headed to the other side of the room.

"Serena, I know I told you before, how beautiful you are. I mean, you're pretty all the time. Today you look glamorous."

A shy smile spread across her mouth. "You're handsome yourself, Mr. Knox."

People mingled over the food and applauded as the newlyweds cut the cake, feeding a slice to each other. The DJ requested the newlyweds begin the first dance. Many couples joined them on the floor, as the married couple finished their dance. The music changed. A fast beat echoed throughout the room.

Adam took Nicky's hand. "Come on, boogie with your old dad."

Nicky eyed Adam and smiled. "This should be fun."

Serena sipped on her punch and grinned at the father and daughter duo as they danced. The song ended and she watched him amble her way.

"I'm not as young as I used to be." Adam huffed, and waved at air in front of his face.

Nicky giggled. "You did okay for an older guy. I'm going to get some more cheese and crackers."

Adam watched his daughter make her way to the buffet table. He turned to Serena as the tune slowed to a romantic song. "Dance with me."

They swayed to the rhythm of a love song. Serena leaned on Adam's shoulder, and felt his head on hers. Her skin tingled with awareness. Serena could feel the thumping. She didn't know if it was her heart pounding or Adams, but she would've sworn if the music stopped, she would hear every beat.

At the last cord of the song, Adam whispered in her ear.

"Could I have this dance for the rest of my life?"

Their eyes met. His stare captivated her. A shaky breath fell on her lips as he enclosed her mouth with his. An announcement directing all the single women to the far side on the room broke the moment of passion as Serena joined a dozen other women.

Betsy's voice sounded with amusement. "Okay, ladies. Here you go." She snickered and leaned back tossing the bouquet into the circle. The flowers curved toward the right and landed in Serena' hands. She clutched the arrangement as her mouth gaped opened.

Nicky almost ran to Adam. "Dad, Serena caught the bouquet." She jumped with excitement and was about to say something else when Serena approached.

Adam looked at the flowers and rubbed his mouth. "You're a good catch."

"It sailed sideways in my direction. I couldn't help but get it after it practically landed in my hands."

Nicky glanced from one adult to another and yawned.

Serena glanced at Nicky and then Adam. "I think you need to get her to the hotel. She looks like she's ready to collapse.

I'm going to say good bye to Betsy. They'll be leaving for the airport."

"You're right. It's been an eventful night for her." Adam paused and glimpsed the flowers in Serena' hand. "Do you need a ride?"

"No, I have Betsy's car. They'll drive Keith's to the airport."

"Okay, I'll pick you up tomorrow before noon. We can have lunch then head home." Adam hugged her and Nicky planted a kiss on her cheek. Serena watched as they headed toward the exit.

SERENA SAW ADAM PULL into the driveway. She checked the lock on Betsy's house to make sure it was secure. Adam got out of the car and loaded her suitcase in the trunk. After they stopped for lunch, the trio headed back to Greensboro. The car was quiet. Nicky had fallen asleep in the back. The radio played low on a contemporary gospel station filling the air with the phrase, you alone are worthy. Adam adjusted the air vent on his side. "I like that singer, so many of his songs remind me the Lord is by our side."

"Yes, He's one of my favorites."

Adam eyed her lovely side view. "Serena, you've made me want to share my life with someone again, our being together, is wonderful."

Serena glanced sideways at Adam. Betsy's words about keeping secrets tugged at her conscience. She needed to tell Adam about the letter. "Jason and Katie...."

Adam shook his head and spoke up quickly. "Serena no. It's okay. We both loved our spouses, but they're gone and I don't think either one of them would want us to live in the past forever."

She was about to explain what she wanted to say when Nicky straightened and pointed to a road sign. "It looks like we're back in Guilford County."

"Yeah, it does" Serena eyed the road sign certain that if her confidence held up. She'd tell Adam about the letter another time. "I enjoyed having you both with me this weekend." She peeked in the rear-view mirror at Nicky.

Adam glanced in the back seat. "It meant a lot to us to be invited, didn't it, Nicky?"

Nicky nodded. "It was a beautiful wedding. I can't wait to tell Jan about the chocolate fondue. And the bouquet Serena caught."

Serena took an exit and then turned into the neighborhood where Adam lived. "It's been a long weekend. I'm sure we're all tired." She stayed in the driver's seat and popped the trunk open.

Adam leaned over, took Serena's chin in his hand, and kissed her. "I'll call you later." He stepped out of the car, grabbed the overnight bags, and waved.

CHAPTER SEVEN

THE NEWLYWEDS WERE home. Betsy emailed Serena pictures of the wedding and the scenery at the Cayman Islands. Serena followed the photo gallery as images flickered across the computer screen, listening while Betsy told her about the Turtle Farm and the beautiful green waters. "You wouldn't believe the cute sandals I got at one of the little gift huts."

Serena chuckled, "I should have known you'd find something to wear."

Betsy joined in on the laughter. "I did and I also got some nice shorts. Look at that snapshot Keith took under the water."

"Oh, it's beautiful. The colors on those coral reefs are so vivid. What camera did you use?"

"I bought him underwater photography equipment as a wedding gift. He enjoys snorkeling. I'm going to mail you photos of the wedding."

"I'll buy frames so I can hang them on the wall. So how's married life, now that you're home and settled in?"

"I'm happy, Serena. I love Keith so much. Each morning he gets up before me, makes coffee, and brings me a cup while I'm getting ready for work. We've started talking about buying a house. Keith's apartment is as old as the hills but we haven't figured out which neighborhood we want to live in yet."

"Don't rush into buying a house. That's a big step."

"I know and I want the home we purchase to be the one we'll live in for a long time. I'd better go. I'm cooking meatloaf for dinner." Betsy laughed. "Keith is a meat and potato's kind of guy. Hey, speaking of men, how are things with you and Adam?"

"Everything's fine." Serena sat back. "I've been on a hectic schedule this week. We've talked on the phone and emailed. Nicky has an outing with the church youth group Saturday, Adam and I plan to spend the day together."

"I'm happy for you. I guess you threw the letter from his late wife away."

"No, I've been busy at the hospital and haven't given it much thought. I almost told him but I can't. I don't know if I have the courage. I'm going to shred it along with some other papers and pretend I never seen that letter."

"That has to be your decision. All I know is that I believe in my heart the Lord guided both of you together, and if he ordains it, then the relationship will work out."

Serena felt a slight tug of guilt. "You'd better go get that man of yours some dinner. We'll talk later."

"NICKY, MAY I SPEAK with you before you go to bed?" Adam called to his daughter as she started to climb the stairs to her room.

"Sure Dad, what's up?"

"Come sit down a minute." Adam patted the couch beside him.

Nicky closed the distance between them and took a seat beside Adam. As he observed his daughter, his mind skipped back to a time when she was younger. Adam smiled as Nicky

sat inches away from him, the little girl of yesterday, replaced by a tender young teenager.

"Dad, why are you looking at me so funny?" Nicky's eyes widened. "Has something happened?"

"I'm sorry honey, I was just remembering back to when you were in elementary school. You were so cute with your long pig tails."

Nicky nodded, "I remember Mom used to like to braid my hair."

"Yes, she said it felt like silk."

"Those were good times Dad." Nicky lowered her head. Her gaze fell to the floor, "I know we aren't supposed to question things, but sometimes I wonder why the Lord called Mom to Heaven. We needed her here."

"I've often had the same thoughts and questions. I don't have the answers. Do you remember how Mom talked about being ready when God calls us home? We know that she was ready."

"Keep Jesus in your heart, Nicky. That's what she always told me." Nicky's head bobbed. "I love you. You've always been there for me. Even when I was acting up, you stood by me.

And you didn't get too mad." She giggled.

"You're my daughter. I love you with all my heart." He patted her hand.

Nicky rested her palm on the top of Adam's hand. "Thanks, Dad. It's you and me, right? Course you're not getting any younger, and one day I'm going to have a busy career like Serena."

Adam smiled. "That's why I wanted to talk with you. I need to speak with you about something and get your input."

Nicky stared at her dad. "Okay, ask."

"Nicky, we're a family and anything I do also affects you. I don't want to make decisions without getting your opinion."

"So, what's up?"

"It's Serena. She's become a big part of my life." Adam cleared his throat. "No one will ever replace your mother, but I know you're old enough to understand that love comes in many different forms."

Nicky's lips spread apart with expectations. "Dad, are you trying to tell me you love Serena?"

"Yes," Adam breathed a sigh. "I also want your permission to ask her to marry me."

Nicky jumped up, leaned down, and flung her arms around Adam's neck.

"Oh, Dad, I love her too!"

Adam returned his daughter's hug.

"Would you help me with something then?"

"Anything, what do you need?" Her eyes sparkled with excitement.

"I have been looking at engagement rings. I found three I like, but I can't decide which one to get. I wanted to propose to her Saturday but I need a ring. Will you go with me after school tomorrow and help me pick one?"

"You got it, Dad! I hope you'll go to that jewelry store that advertises the special diamond cuts. They are all so beautiful there."

Adam chuckled at Nicky's comment. "Is there any other store in Greensboro?"

Nicky hugged Adam again, before she ran up the steps.

THEY SAT AT THE BURGER Hut. Adam took the wrapper off a Chicken Filet sandwich and Nicky took a bite from the burger she'd ordered.

"Nicky, I'm glad you're okay with me asking Serena to be part of our family."

"I'm happy you and Serena found each other."

"Well, if Serena agrees to marry me, our life will be different, but I want you to understand, I love you. You've always been my first priority and that won't change."

"Dad, I know. I think that Serena will fit in just fine." They finished the meal and Adam drove to the mall.

NICKY STOOD BESIDE Adam at Zelman's Fine Jewelry. Upon seeing the three rings, she immediately pushed one ring back.

"This one's just plain Dad, it only has one diamond."

Adam watched Nicky discard the diamond solitaire. The sales clerk placed it in the case and eyed Adam with curiosity.

"My daughter is helping me choose the proper ring."

"I see," the clerk nodded toward Nicky. "I'm sure she'll be a lot of help."

Nicky was straight-faced as she turned a ring around looking at it from different angles. "What's the difference in these rings?" She held two choices up to examine each one.

"Well, one is called a Halo ring and the other," the clerk pointed to the ring Nicky held. "See the way the small gems run down the sides, highlighting the large stone of top." The attentive woman touched a stone on the shank. "This one is a square frame diamond."

Nicky looked closer, "Dad, I think Serena will like this one. Look at the way the little diamonds make a box around the big one." She handed the diamond to Adam.

"Yes, I like this one too."

Adam handed the ring back to the clerk. "We'll take it."

The woman smiled. "What size do you need?"

Adam turned his attention to the corner of the store and then looked back at the sales clerk. "I'm afraid I don't know."

"Wait a minute," Nicky chimed in. "When Serena and I were cooking I put my ring on her finger, and it only went to here." She placed her finger on her other hand indicating the stopping point.

The sales woman reached out to Nicky, "Let me see your ring, perhaps we can get it close." She glanced at Adam for his approval. "If it doesn't fit exactly right you can bring it back for sizing later."

AN HOUR LATER ADAM and Nicky walked into the house. "Dad, I think that ring is beautiful."

"I hope Serena likes it."

"She will, you'll see. All day Saturday while I'm at the zoo, I'm going to be thinking about this. I hope she says, yes. It would be nice to have Serena living with us."

Adam kissed Nicky on the check. "I want her to say yes too."

"I'm going up to bed now, night, Dad" Nicky skipped up the stairs with visions of the perfect wedding in her mind.

ADAM SAT IN THE LIVING room at Serena's house sipping a glass of tea. He watched as his love maneuvered the siphon hose to drain a few gallons of water from the tank. "Are you sure you don't want me to do that?"

"No, I can do it. It's easy, I just use the hose to drain half of the water and this tool which looks like a meat baste and remove some of the dirt from the bottom."

Adam rose and stepped behind Serena. He closed his arms around her. "You're a wonderful lady. I've had a good time with you today."

"Yeah, I'll bet you enjoyed helping me shop for picture frames and a paper shredder," her voice sounded pleasant, but hesitant.

Adam hugged her. "I like shopping with you anytime." He turned her to face him. "Serena, I could enjoy doing anything as long as you're by my side, let me help you clean that tank, we have dinner reservations soon."

"I'm finished, except for adding more water and putting the fish back in the tank, but I do need to change my clothes and freshen up." She held out the jug for him.

He took the water from Serena. "I'll finish this-you go and get dressed."

Adam smiled as Serena walked to her bedroom and closed the door. He poured water in the tank, replaced the fish, and then turned on the aquarium light to observe the large goldfish. As it swam close to the edge he said, "Well little Adam, wish me luck tonight."

Serena returned to the living room. "I'm ready." She smiled, clothed in a sleeveless mauve dress, a gold cross necklace-hung from her neck.

Adam's eyes rose in appreciation. She was dressed for a special occasion. He hoped that a marriage proposal would be unique enough.

MUSIC FLOWED THROUGH the room in the dining area. The soft tunes created a relaxing atmosphere. They sat at a table in the back of the room. Light from decorative chandeliers shined on the wall and provided a glow over the table. The waiter took away their empty plates. The main meal was gone, now strawberries, and Bavarian pie sat before them. "Adam, the Steak Carpaccio was delicious!" "It was good." He took a bite of his pie.

Serena watched him. She was full, but the pleasure on his face made her stretch out her fork and stab at a piece of the luscious fruit.

"This is a nice restaurant. I've enjoyed our day together."

Adam wiped his mouth on a napkin and reached across the table for her hand.

"Serena, if today is a glimpse of life with you. I want it forever." He released her hand, reached into his pocket, and took out the ring box. "I truly believe the Lord sent you to me. I love you with all my heart and want you to be my wife."

Serena stared at Adam and then eyed the ring. The three-quarter square diamond surrounded by small stones, sparkled. She put her hand to her mouth and continued to glance at the ring and Adam, unable to speak.

Several seconds of silence passed. Adam fidgeted, and finally spoke. "Serena?"

Serena looked at Adam. A timid grin passed between them.

"Adam, there's a lot to consider, it's not just the two of us. There's more to it."

"I only have one question. Do you love me?"

His words echoed in her ears. She nodded her head. "Yes, I love you."

"Then what's stopping us from becoming a family? All the other things can be worked out. I talked to Nicky a few days ago." Adam touched her fingers with his. "She loves you and wants us to be together." He took the ring out of the box and began to slip it on her finger.

"I love you, be my wife."

Serena let Adam place the ring on her finger. She held her hand close and admired the setting. "Yes, I want to be with you forever."

Adam lips parted in a wide smiled as he held Serena's hand and sealed the union with a kiss.

SERENA AND ADAM STOOD inside the foyer of her condominium. Adam drew her close to him. The kisses they shared lingered. Each one grew more passionate. Serena moved back. "I love you, Adam."

Adam pulled her close and fondled her hair. "I want to be with you. When can we get married?"

Serena turned her head sideways, contemplating the question. "Why don't we start the new year off as man and wife?

We can marry at the end of December."

Adam pouted. "I was hoping we could get married in a couple weeks, but I know you women, with all your plans." He chuckled.

"Two weeks? Adam, do you realize December is only three months away. I will be very busy getting everything ready by then! I plan to include Nicky in everything. Then, there is my mother. I'd like to take you and Nicky to meet her before the ceremony. She lives in a retirement facility close by."

Adam held his hand up. "Okay, you win. I'll be patient. And I want to meet my future mother-in-law." Adam kissed her. "I'm counting the weeks until you become Mrs. Knox."

Serena watched Adam pull out of the driveway. She walked to the bedroom, gathered her nightclothes, and after a quick shower slipped under the covers. A few seconds later, she got up and knelt beside the bed. "Lord, help me to do your will. Bless Adam and me as we start a new life together and watch over Nicky. In Jesus name I pray, Amen."

CHAPTER EIGHT

SERENA WOKE WITH THE sun peeping through the curtains. She dressed and grabbed the cell phone as she went into the kitchen to prepare coffee. The beverage dripped into the decanter while she pressed the button to place a call.

"Betsy, how's your morning?"

"I'm on my way to work. You never call this early, what's up?"

"Oh, nothing much, I just wanted to tell you that Adam asked me to marry him last night and I want you to be my matron of honor."

"Okay." Betsy turned into the parking deck searching for a space, a second later it dawned on her what Serena said. "Goodness. He proposed?"

"Yes, that's what I said." She poured a cup of coffee.

"Girl, tell me all about it."

Betsy sat in her car and listened as Serena recapped her date with Adam. "I told him I wanted to get married after Christmas, I'm thinking December twenty-eight. School is out so Adam will have time off. We can spend a few days somewhere tropical for a honeymoon and then start the New Year off as a married couple."

"Serena, I'm happy for you. I told you this was meant to be."

"I'm still in shock. Betsy, my life has changed so much this year."

"Yes, it has. I think it's about time you found a new love. The Lord works in his own wonderful way." Betsy got out of the car and shut the door. "I have to clock in. I'll call you this evening. We have plans to make."

Serena ended the call and filled her cup again. It was her day off so she worked around the house until noon, then placed her laptop on the table, made a club sandwich, and searched for Bridal Gowns on the internet. I can't believe I'm looking at wedding dresses. Serena bookmarked a site, which had a dress she liked. She wanted to show it to Nicky.

The phone buzzed.

"Hello, beautiful, what are you doing?"

"Adam, hi. I just finished lunch. How are things at school?"

"Fine, it's actually been a quiet day. I was hoping you'd be free tonight. Nicky and I would like you to come to dinner."

"Sounds good, what's the plan?"

"Nicky wants to cook for you. She's fixing that macaroni dish you taught her, and I'm cooking a ham."

"Well, I can't turn that down, it sounds wonderful!" "Let me warn you, Nicky's armed with magazines." "Magazines?" Serena wrinkled her brow.

"Yeah, those bride catalogs you women buy. She picked several up at the grocery store."

"Nicky wants to talk wedding plans. I'm glad she's happy about us. I want her to feel that she's a big part of our lives."

"She's excited, probably not as much as her dad. Serena I can't wait for us to be man and wife. Which reminds me, I need to ask you something?" Silence filled the air as Adam hesitated.

"Adam, what do you want to ask?"

"I know we only got engaged yesterday and haven't had an opportunity to discuss much, but I wanted to know how you felt about living with me and Nicky... or if you rather, we buy a house together?"

"I haven't really thought about it. Maybe, we can live at your place for a while and then we can pick out a new home later, if we want. That way, Nicky can adjust to everything."

"I knew you would have the perfect solution. I love you. I'll see you around six."

NICKY MET SERENA AT the door. "Come on in, dinner's ready. I have magazines and a note pad. We can start planning the wedding. Dad said that you guys are getting married after Christmas, that's not far away."

Serena followed Nicky into the living room, happy about the girl's enthusiasm. "Only a few months, you think we can organize everything by then?"

Nicky smiled. "Sure! We can start by making notes tonight, and when we're done with each thing, we can mark them off the list."

"Wow, you would make a good wedding coordinator." Serena glanced into the dining room and noticed the table set with fine China. Adam stepped from the kitchen and moved towards Serena.

"I'm glad you came tonight." He escorted her to the table and pulled out the chair for her.

"Everything looks wonderful." Serena glanced at the food. "Did you make the potato salad?"

"No, it's store bought. I haven't been able to master the right ingredients yet." Adam pulled out Nicky's chair, and then he took a seat. In habit, everyone bowed while he petitioned the Lord, "Heavenly Father, bless this bounty before us, Amen."

After the meal and ice cream for dessert, they all sat in the living room. Serena relaxed on the couch between Nicky and Adam.

Nicky had a magazine spread out showing Serena the latest styles in bridal dresses and flower arrangements.

"What do you think about this one, Serena?" Nicky pointed to a Silk A-line dress.

"I like that, but I think this one would look better on me. She examined a selection of dresses with sleeves on the other page. "This has a Tulle Jacket with lace embroidery, and I need an ivory color."

Nicky studied the picture. "Why do you want an ivory wedding dress?"

"I've been married before. Ivory is the customary color."

"Even, if your husband died?"

"If it's a second marriage, ivory is the most common shade. Anyway, we can't pick a dress from this book."

Nicky looked at the pages and glanced back at Serena, "Why not?"

Serena put her arm around Nicky and hugged her. "Your Dad can't see the dress until the day of the wedding. We're going to have to go shopping without him and pick out the gown."

Adam listened to the wedding talk. "Okay ladies, I can tell I'm not wanted," he laughed.

Serena reached for his hand and squeezed it gently. Her eyes captured his. "You're very much wanted. I can't wait for the day I'll walk down the aisle to you." Her cheeks blushed at her own comment.

Nicky watched Adam lean over and kiss Serena. She shook her head. "Okay guys, I'm going upstairs, Serena when are we going to go shopping?"

"Well... The dresses and the flowers are the preparations we can decide on. Why don't you and I go to the bridal shop in a couple of weeks? I need to see if Betsy can go with us. Later, we both can pick out flower arrangements."

Nicky stood and kissed Adam goodnight, then she leaned toward Serena, offered a hug, and planted a kiss on her cheek.

"Sounds good, just let me know what time."

Adam and Serena watched Nicky go upstairs. Adam scooted closer to Serena. "I enjoyed tonight and Nicky's on cloud nine."

Adam started on her neck and seductively trailed a line of kisses to her lips. After several passionate embraces, he released her. "I don't know what I would have done if you said no. I love you and can't imagine life without you."

The next hour passed. Adam and Serena talked about their life together. Adam scooted to the edge of the couch and eyed the magazine lying on the coffee table. "I'll get some tea. We can go over Nicky's list and make some plans of our own."

"You sure you want to do it now." Serena picked up the notepad.

"We need to start planning. Like you said, three months isn't long." He stood, "course if you want, we can always trash the catalogue, grab Nicky, and find a Justice of the Peace." He watched Serena's eyes get wider. "Seriously, this wedding is important to me, and a church ceremony is nice. I'm only playing." He left to get the beverages.

Adam returned with glasses of sweetened tea and handed one to Serena. She took a sip before she sat her drink down.

"Maybe we can get married at Salvation's Door. They have a large recreation space across the street for functions. Will that be good for the reception?"

"Yes, that sounds fine to me. It'll be nice to get married in a church."

Serena listened to the odd tone of his voice as he commented about being married in a house of worship. She couldn't remember if he had mentioned his first wedding. "You and Katie weren't married in a church?"

"No, you know how it is; we were young and planned a family fast." Adam saw the questioning look in Serena's eyes. He sat down his drink. "It's a long story. I promise to tell you about it later. Right now, I want to concentrate on our lives together." He pulled her close.

The comments he made bounced around in Serena's mind. She wanted to ask about the quick wedding. She longed to know if Adam realized he wasn't Nicky's parental father. Serena opened her mouth to speak, but couldn't decide how to bring up the subject. She then recalled her decision to trash the letter and forget it all. "We can speak to Pastor Bob, and see what he says."

"Okay, that's a plan." He kissed her.

Serena gladly returned his caress. As they parted, she noticed the hour on the wall clock. "I'd better go. We both have a busy day at work tomorrow."

AFTER THE HOSPITAL rounds Serena met Carole outside for the afternoon break. They took seats in the gazebo. Carole tore open a candy bar wrapper. A sparkle coming from the stone on Serena's finger caught her eye. She reached for Serena's hand.

"Is that what I think it is? You're engaged!"

Serena grinned as Carole held on to her fingers. "Yes, Adam purposed a few days ago. We've been so busy I'd forgotten to mention it."

Carole chewed a bite of the chocolate and smiled. "How could you forget that?"

"I don't know." Serena leaned back. "I'm sorry. We've decided to have the ceremony December twenty-eighth."

The women began walking to the entrance of the hospital.

"I know a great caterer." Carole tossed the empty candy wrapper in the trash bin." She does a fine job, and the food is delicious."

"That sounds good-give me her phone number, and I'll call her."

As Serena's workday ended, things in the children's wing slowed down. Several young patients had gone home. The rooms were clean and prepped for new arrivals.

She left the hospital, pulled into a drive-thru, ordered a burger and salad. When she walked in to her condominium, she took off her shoes and went into the kitchen with the food. As she opened the container full of salad, she pressed the button on her cell to call Betsy.

"Hi, Serena, how was your day?"

"It was good, five children were discharged today. How was your day?" Serena removed the wrapper from her sandwich.

"I had a pleasant day, not a lot of sickness in the ER and that's good! What plans for the wedding are you working on?"

Serena swallowed. "Nicky is anxious to go shopping for a wedding dress. I told her we'd go in a couple of weeks. Do you think you, and Keith can come to Greensboro? I'd like you to go with us. I want my matron of honor my junior bridesmaid with me when I pick out a dress. That is, if I can find a dress in one day. She laughed

"I'll speak to Keith about it, and see if we can schedule coinciding days off for that weekend. I have a couple of people who owe me time-off for working for them. I'll let you know."

"Great, I'm going to need your help."

"Serena, you sound nervous."

"I am a little. I don't know what lies ahead and that has me a bit flustered."

"None of us do, that's the good thing about having a relationship with Jesus Christ. He will see us through the unknown."

"You're right, Betsy."

SUNDAY ADAM AND NICKY stopped by Serena's house. She rode with them to church. Nicky went to youth class and

Serena sat beside Adam as the preacher spoke about living for Christ. Adam listened to the leader of the church.

"Congregation, it is important to be the kind of person the Lord's wants us to be at all times. The world will try us, but we must stand strong with the grace God gives his children. Turn to Galatians 5:22-13. Let's talk about the fruits of the spirit."

The service ended and Adam and Serena asked the preacher if they could speak with him.

"Come to my office." He led them down the hall to the back of the church. After everyone was seated, he asked, "How may I help?"

Adam cleared his throat. "Pastor Bob, Serena, and I are getting married December twenty-eight and we'd like you to marry us. We hope the date is available."

The pastor looked at the couple and smiled. "If I remember correctly, I don't have anything scheduled in December except for our church Christmas program and my wife is usually the leader of that event. I'll write it on my calendar. Next month, we'll get together and discuss all the plans. I'm sure our piano player Martha, would enjoy performing the wedding march for the ceremony,"

Serena tightened her grip on Adam's hand and grinned. "That will be wonderful. Would it be okay if we booked our reception in the banquet hall across the street?"

"Of course, I expect you too."

"Thank you."

They stood and Adam shook the man's hand. As they were leaving, he pulled Serena close for a hug. "It's all working out nicely."

They waited on Nicky and they all took their place in the car headed to a restaurant.

Adam, Serena, and Nicky sat at the square table in the middle of eating establishment. During the meal, they discussed the wedding. Serena glanced around at the half-dozen tables which remained occupied. Serena put her fork into the slice of apple pie and then turned her attention to Nicky. "Betsy is coming down in a couple of weeks, and we'll go shopping for our dresses. She will need a gown for the matron of honor, and you'll need a bridesmaid dress."

Nicky twisted her face in thought. "What's the difference between a bride's maid and a matron of honor?"

Adam wiped a smudge of chocolate mousse from his mouth. "I can answer this one. A bride's maid is usually single."

"Oh, okay. Well, I guess we're doing things right." Nicky spooned banana pudding into her mouth.

"Nicky, you're very special to me, I love you." Serena touched Nicky's hand on the table. "You're going to be a beautiful bride's maid."

Nicky held Serena's fingers a moment before turning them loose. "I'm happy we're going to become a family. I still love my mom, but it will be nice having you around as a mom too."

Like a hot drink on a cold day, the words Nicky said coated Serena's heart in warmth. She spread her mouth in a wide grin and nodded. "I've never had children. You're just like a daughter to me." She watched Nicky's smile beam in agreement and then focus on her pudding.

"Adam, Keith will be coming to Greensboro with Betsy."

"Good, I can use the reinforcements. Keith and I will watch some sports on television. I may even start the grill and barbeque. After you, ladies finish shopping, we all can enjoy a mini-cook out."

Serena laughed, "You're fond of that grill, but it's a great idea."

THE BLARING HORN DREW Serena's attention. She glanced outside and saw Betsy and Keith get out of the car. Serena opened the door as they approached the steps. "Hi, you're early." I wasn't

expecting you two for another hour."

"I wanted to get started early." Keith followed Serena into the house.

"Yes, he woke me up at five." Betsy glanced at her husband and grinned.

"Look ladies, I know how women are when they shop. I figured if you got to the store when it opened maybe, you would get done today."

Betsy and Serena gazed at each other and then laughed.

"He's very optimistic. Come in, Keith. I'll show you where the guest room is and you can unpack."

"Since we're here, I suppose we can grab a quick breakfast and head to the mall." Betsy opened the luggage and hung a pair of pants in the closet.

"Yes, we can. I'll call Adam and make sure Nicky will be ready. After breakfast, we can pick her up. I've got coffee on, let's go to the kitchen."

"Will Adam and I stay at his house while you ladies go shopping?" Keith poured some of the coffee in a mug.

"Yes, if that's okay with you. Adam said something about sports on TV."

Keith nodded his head in Serena's direction, "Great, I would rather watch a game anytime than shop for dresses." He reached out and hugged Betsy.

"Funny guy," Betsy jokingly slapped him on the arm.

"I'll call the Knox's house and let Nicky know what time we're coming." Serena walked toward the living room. "And then I'll fix French toast."

THE HOUSE WAS BUZZING with noise. Adam and Keith were discussing the game and Serena was platting Nicky's hair. Betsy watched her secure the style.

"Okay, we're ready." Nicky patted her braid.

"Let's go! We may not get back until later this evening." Betsy raised her voice as they walked to the front door.

Keith and Adam met them in the entryway before they went outside. "We'll be fine. Serena, call me when you three get ready to leave the store. 'll fire-up the grill." Adam kissed Serena and hugged his daughter.

THE WOMEN LOOKED IN four stores before Serena decided to try on dresses at Don's Bridal Mark.

"There so many choices. I don't know which one to choose." Nicky's eyes moved from one gorgeous dress to another. As the women chose their attire, Nicky added. "I'm taking pictures with my phone in case we can't decide today."

The bridal consultant led them to a dressing room and left a bell to ring if they needed her.

"I like this empire, knee length chiffon, Nicky." Betsy fanned the dress out.

"I do too. It's wonderful on you." Serena hung one of the outfits back on a hanger.

Nicky looked at the choices. "Okay, I agree, this one is best. What about you two."

Betsy gazed at the clothes set out in the private dressing hall. "Since Serena's colors are gold and ivory, I believe I like this gold A-line tea length dress, with the lace."

Serena removed a veil for a hanger. "Yes, it's beautiful, Betsy. I can't believe both of you found a perfect fit, and I have to come back and get mine altered." Serena pretended to pout.

"I know, but Serena the ivory gown with the pleated front, the cap sleeves, and the beads will be just right on you."

"It's pretty. I like the way the beads are made into the sleeves." Nicky moved sideways in front of the three-way mirror.

Serena took one more look at the outfits hanging from the hooks. "I agree. This is a wonderful dress. I'll schedule a time to get it hemmed. Let's tell the bridal consultant we've made our decisions."

They strolled through the parking lot after a day of shopping. Betsy walked on the other side of Nicky.

The women seated themselves inside the car and Serena turned on the main road toward Adam's house. "Nicky call Adam and tell him we're on our way."

WHEN THEY WALKED OUT to the patio Adam and Keith were talking about team scores. Keith turned and saw Betsy. "It's about time you got back. I thought I was going to have to move in with Adam." He hugged his wife.

"I told you we were going to try and find our wedding attire today."

"And did you?" Adam walked to Serena and planted a kiss on her lips.

"We did, even found shoes to match." Serena seated herself next to Nicky.

Laughter filled the kitchen. Everyone chatted while eating chicken wings and hotdogs. Later, the women cleaned the kitchen, and the men took care of the grill.

Keith and Adam came from the deck back into the house as Serena glanced at her watch. "I guess we'd better go. I didn't realize how late it was getting."

"You're right." Keith threw a paper plate in the trash.

Serena, Betsy, and Keith moved towards the front door.

Adam followed and shook Keith's hand. "It's not often I get to debate sports." Come back and watch the game with me anytime."

"Hey man, we'll do it again," Keith agreed.

Nicky walked over and hugged Serena and then Betsy. "I had fun shopping and we're all going to be so beautiful. Especially you, Serena."

Serena put her finger on her lips. "Remember, mum's the word about my dress."

"Not a problem." Nicky made an imaginary x on her chest to promise.

Keith and Betsy got into the car. Serena stood on the porch with Adam.

"Keith is a nice guy, I'm glad he came."

"I'm glad you both get along. I don't have to worry about you not liking my best friend's husband."

"Will I see you tomorrow?"

"I don't know. I promised to take them to the hospital where I work, before they leave for Wilmington. You know we're all in the medical field, I figured I'd show them one of the hospitals in Greensboro, you're welcome to come along."

"Keith sounds like a smart man. He enlightened me on the responsibilities of the hospital lab. It's a lot more complicated than I would have thought, but I'll let you and your friends get caught up with all the medical jargon." He embraced Serena in a long kiss. "Can I take you out Saturday night? Nicky is going to the movies with her friend. The girl's mom is taking them for pizza and then a show."

"I'll be ready and waiting." She smiled and turned to leave.

"I can't wait until you become my wife." Adam reluctantly let her go.

SERENA TOOK KEITH AND Betsy out for breakfast and then they toured Long Pine Hospital. She introduced them to Carole and several staff members and they drove back to Serena's place.

"Keith, I enjoyed having you here. Adam did too."

"It was fun, I like your fiancé."

Keith called to Betsy. "I'll load the car and give you and Serena time to say your goodbyes."

Betsy watched him stroll to the car with the overnight bags.

"That's a nice hospital you work at."

"I like it. The people are great. Betsy I'm glad I made this move. So many positive things have happened."

"Yes, you have a job working with children every day. I know that's something you've always wanted and a wonderful man. You'll soon be Mrs. Adam Knox." Betsy hugged Serena.

"I'm glad you made peace with the letter."

Serena walked with her friend to the front door. "I wouldn't say I'm at harmony about the contents of the note, but I don't know if saying anything is right either. I'm off work Saturday I plan to shred it along with some old receipts."

"I'm sure everything will be fine. Call me." Betsy hugged Serena and then trotted down the steps. She headed to the car waving good-bye.

CHAPTER NINE

SATURDAY, AFTER SERENA ate breakfast, she worked in her flower garden. At twelve, she grabbed a quick lunch. As the day wore, Serena took a bottle of water from the refrigerator and stood in front of the double doors that led to her patio. She admired the trees in a distance as the limbs swayed in the breeze. All the foliage is so pretty this time of the year. Serena turned around as a notion sprang to her mind. Those documents need shredding. She took the last sip of water and tossed the plastic in the recycle bin, speaking aloud Serena reconfirmed her decision.

"I'll destroy that letter. Nothing would be accomplished by telling them."

Standing in the hall, Serena grabbed a boot box from the top shelf filled with old warranties for small appliances from years past. She peeked inside and noticed the dates on the papers were past expiration. She closed the lid and reached for the tattered envelope she'd stashed on the top shelf.

Serena carried the carton to the living room setting it on the end table. She took a seat on the couch. Her hand tightly grasped the envelope as she read the front. One last time she took out the page and stared at the words Katie had written to Jason. Placing the letter down beside her, Serena began to sort through the other documents. She guided the ones she didn't want between the teeth of the machine and watched as tiny strips fell from the other side.

Serena worked feeding one paper, then another until she'd accumulated a piled of confetti then switched off the shredder and emptied the plastic canister into the trash.

Back in the living room, she grabbed a stack of old newspaper clippings and once again fed the paper eating apparatus. Her eyes glanced at the letter which she planned to shred last.

Suddenly Serena's cell phone chimed and broke her concentration.

"Hi beautiful what are you doing?" Adam's smooth voice flowed to her ears.

"I'm making use of that paper shredder, and tearing up a bunch of old receipts. It's one of those things I've neglected. What are you up to?"

"Nothing now, earlier I finished some housework, and shopped for groceries. Nicky can put away the food."

"Adam, she's young. It's a known fact teenagers eat constantly."

"I know. I'm not complaining."

"You're a wonderful dad."

"Thanks, sometimes I need a vote of confidence on my side." Adam's voice changed to a lower tone. "I can't wait to see you later. After dinner, do you want to watch a movie at my place? That way I'll be here when Nicky gets back from her friend's house. We'll drive you home."

Serena glanced at the clock and frowned at way the morning hours had seemed to rush by. "That sounds. I'll be ready."

"Okay, I'll see you in about an hour."

Serena pushed the button to end the call. I'd better get in the shower. She jumped from the sofa and headed to her bedroom.

She unplugged her curling iron and finished her hair. The doorbell rang and Serena may her way from the bedroom to the living room to open the door. "Hi, come in. I need to get my shoes and I'll be ready."

"Okay, I'll wait right here."

Adam kissed her and watched her bare feet take brisk steps toward the hall. He moseyed to the fish tank and peeked in the glass at the Neon's swimming, then sat down on the sofa. He glanced at the paper shredder and the typed forms lying on the coffee table and remembered Serena mentioned destroying old receipts. As he waited, his attention fluttered to a handwritten letter which rested on the sofa.

Adam looked away, not wanting to be nosy. He tried to ignore the fact that the writing on that old letter seemed familiar? As if he couldn't control his eyes his focus went back on

the note. A signature came into view. "Katie."

Adam heard Serena and started to stand, but noticed the worn message again. As if the page was alive, the name Nicky seemed to jump to from the paper. It's a coincidence. Before he considered his actions of invading Serena's privacy, he picked up the letter and read.

Serena tossed a pair of low heels in the closet and then tried on another pair before deciding on her wedge sandals. Finally, she was ready. She walked into the living room, and saw Adam standing rigid. His face laced with anger.

Serena looked at his pasty white complexion and his eyes narrowed to a slit. As she wondered what was wrong her gaze then fell to his hand. He had the letter fisted in a tight hold.

"Serena, what is this?" Adam's words came out laced with venom as he held up the note.

"Adam, I can explain." Serena touched her throat and swallowed.

"Really, this ought to be good!" Adam's words echoed in the room. His nostril flared.

"This is Katie's writing, and she's talking about our daughter." Adam gritted his teeth. "Where did you get this? And this Jason. Was he your husband?"

"Adam, please sit down. Let me explain." Her voice trembled. but she held back her emotions.

"No, I'll stand... You talk." He nodded to the paper still in his hand.

"Jason was my husband. Nicky's real father. I wanted to tell you, but I fell in love with you, and then I didn't want to hurt either of you." She hugged her arms as she responded. "I was planning to destroy the letter, so no one would be hurt."

"So, you've had this all along and didn't mention it," he admonished.

"I didn't know what to do. There was no reason to say anything." Serena slumped on the corner of the couch. "Both Jason and Katie are gone. You're all that Nicky has left."

Adam glared at her. "Am I to believe that this letter, you and I, our love.... It's all coincidence?"

"Yes," Serena stated firmly. "I wasn't searching for you. I didn't plan to meet you, and I assure you, my love is real." She stood and took a step towards him.

"Hah, I don't know what's true anymore." Adam stepped back. "That's a sorry explanation."

Serena held her head up. "It's all I have. The truth. The letter arrived months after I lost Jason. Katie obviously didn't know about Jason's accident. I guess she was reaching out to him, before her own death. I've tried to bring it up to you several times, but the moment never seemed right. I decided to forget about it. I was planning to destroy it."

"And you just happened to move here? Just coincidently come to my school, met Nicky, and give her your email?" His jaw wiggled as he spat out the accusing words.

"Yes, I moved to Greensboro because my mother has Alzheimer's. I agreed to go the Ms. Hardy's class in Carole's place. I can't even begin to tell you how shocked I was the day I met Nicky, and then you." She twisted her hands as she talked.

"Since then, you've had plenty of time to tell me about this. What kept you from sharing the letter?" Adam demanded, "Something so important."

"I wasn't sure if you knew you weren't Nicky's biological father. I saw how much she loves you and I didn't want to stand in the way of the relationship you two have. It could have hurt you and Nicky to find out if you didn't already know. Then when we fell in love, I didn't know what to do." Serena exhaled a shaky breath. "Adam, I didn't want to lose you."

"Sounds farfetched and doesn't set well." He watched Serena. His mind teetered with indecision. "If this is all so innocent, you should have told me."

"Yes, I needed to, I'm sorry," her voice barely above a whisper. Her eyes brimmed with tears.

"Katie never told me the name of Nicky's real father." Adam spoke as if he was alone in the room. Then his words grew angry again.

"She made a mistake Serena and got pregnant. That is the reason we married so soon. Regardless, of that, I loved her. I wanted to set things right for the child. Later, I asked her if she thought about telling Nicky's father. Katie said she didn't know where he moved."

In one fast movement, Adam tossed the letter down, move to the door and opened his exit. "If you care anything for Nicky, you'll keep this information to yourself. One day, I'm going to tell her everything, but I figure she's entitled to grow up with a happy childhood. At least, as good as it can be without a mother. Like you said, Jason's dead, he can't be a father, but I can." He pointed to his chest.

"Of course." Serena nodded

Adam gave Serena a cold stare. "As for us, I won't live with a woman who keeps things from me." The door slammed.

Serena hung her head and squeezed her eyes tight in an effort to hold back the tears that flowed. The sound of her sobs echoed throughout the room.

After her tears spent, Serena pushed off the sofa, ambled to the bathroom, blew her nose, and splashed cold water on her swollen face. The sad reflection gawked at her from the mirror. Her limp body moved in turtle speed to her bedroom. She reached for the phone and called Betsy.

"SERENA, WHAT'S WRONG? You sound upset."

"I made a horrible mistake, Betsy. I should have listened to you!" Serena sniffed, and focused on an embellished swirl pattern on the chair, trying to keep tears from flowing again. "Serena, what happened?" Betsy urged.

"I accidentally left that blasted letter on the couch. Adam came and saw it. He is mad that I hid it from him. I tried to explain my reasons, but now he said he can't be with anyone who keeps secrets."

A gasp came from the phone, "Oh no, Serena. I'm sorry. You have to talk to Adam some more, make him understand why you didn't say anything."

"It's no use I really hurt the trust he had in me."

"Serena, I don't know what to say. Maybe, when things clear a little he'll see it your way."

"I'll pray for you, this situation looks hopeless, but God can turn things around. We have to stand in faith. I've told you that I believe you two are meant to be together."

"I remember. Betsy, I love him so much, but he thinks he can't trust me. He won't give me another chance."

"Serena. Adam loves you. Let him think things over. In the meantime, we'll pray."

"Yeah," Serena replied with no hope in her voice. "I'll talk to you tomorrow."

Serena walked into the living room. She gazed at the stack of papers. Her mind wasn't on finishing the task so she shoved forms back in to the box. The letter lay on the floor. She tossed it into the carton with the other documents and placed everything in the hall closet.

THE ENGAGEMENT RING rested in a small padded manila envelope.

Serena placed it in her purse and drove to the school on her way home. In the administration office, she approached the secretary. "I would like to see Mr. Knox, please."

"I'm sorry, but he is in a meeting. He won't be available for at least an hour. Is there something I can help you with?"

Serena looked around, made a decision and reached inside her purse. "Please, give this to him for me. It's very important."

"I'll see that he gets this when he returns." The woman grinned and took the envelope.

SERENA SAT ON THE COUCH with her legs propped on the coffee table. The laptop rested on her knees. She read a message from Betsy and responded. Nicky's email was next. She wrote several times since Serena and Adam broke up. Every message ended the same way. Nicky asked what was wrong. Serena's reply was always vague. Once more, she sat in front of her computer and looked at the concerned words from a young teenage girl. She jotted a response,

"Nicky, everything is fine with me. I miss you too. Always remember I love you, but often adults get into situations beyond their control. Just because Adam and I aren't together doesn't change the fact that I'm your forever friend."

Later, that night as Serena tossed in bed, she clasped her hands together. "Lord, you know I love Adam. I thought we were supposed to be together, but if not, I'll move on and wait for the person you have destined for me. Keep me safe in your arms, guide me, and help me to move past this. Amen."

The next morning, Serena woke to the birds chirping. She opened her blinds, and searched the back yard for the colorful feathered flyers. Daylight began and hope brewed deep within her heart. She stretched and turned away from the window.

"Lord, I have to believe that you have good things planned for me, I trust you."

CHAPTER TEN

ADAM AND NICKY FINISHED dinner. Nicky slowly wiped the counter top while Adam stacked plates in the dishwasher.

"Dad, that yellow envelope that was on the hall table last week, I looked inside. It was Serena's ring." "Yes," Adam mumbled.

"Why?" Nicky's high-pitched question filled the kitchen. "Can't you two work things out?"

"Nicky, we talked about this the other day." Adam watched his daughter's face as his voice pleaded for her to understand. "I can't explain it all right now. Perhaps one day, I will. Grown people often face situations such as this. Things change."

Nicky threw the dishtowel down and put her hands on her hips, "Dad, I'm tired of that old explanation. Answer me one thing, will you?"

Adam nodded. "What is it?"

"Do you still love Serena enough to marry her?"

Adam's lip wiggled as he blew out a breath. "I love Serena and if things weren't complicated..." He stepped closer to Nicky and spoke in a defeated tone. "You know we would get married."

"Grown-ups make things harder than they should," Nicky crossed her arms. "You've always told me to tackle one challenge at a time, to break down the problem into simple steps.

Maybe, if you look at it differently."

"Nicky, this isn't a math problem," Adam interrupted her in a dismissive tone.

Nicky stomped out of the kitchen and headed up the stairs. Her voice floated down as the noise from her footsteps increased.

"I think you're scared, Dad! Nothing is perfect. People aren't either. You told me that. Serena loves you and you love her."

The last thing Adam heard before she slammed her bedroom door was, "we could have been a family."

Adam dropped into the chair and bowed his head. "Lord, I didn't want this to happen. I love Serena, but she kept something important from me. I have to protect Nicky. Heavenly

Father, I need you to show me the answer."

SATURDAY ADAM WOKE and stared at the ceiling. His mind wandered to possibilities, if only things were different. Why did she keep the fact that her late husband is Nicky's real father from me? He slapped his knee "Is it possible the whole thing is a coincidence?" In spite of all his misgivings, Adam sat on the side of the bed and daydreamed about Serena.

His eyes searched the room and stopped on an antique armoire in the corner, the one piece of furniture that hadn't been opened since Katie's death, He stared at it and recalled that he had planned to look inside and clean it out over a year ago.

Adam dressed and walked to the kitchen to fix a bowl of cereal. Nicky stood against the counter eating fruity flakes and watched him. He poured milk over a bowl of toasted oats.

"Nicky, come sit a minute."

Nicky rolled her eyes. "Every time you say that, it means we need to talk."

Adam grinned, "I guess it does."

Nicky took a seat across from her dad. "And?"

"Nicky, I can't offer a good explanation right now concerning the decision I made about marrying Serena. She wasn't honest with me about something that I think is important in our relationship. It broke the trust I had for her. I need to have confidence in the woman I marry. I hope you'll forgive me. I never intended to tear us apart by this. I want you to be happy."

"You said you love her. Why can't you give her another chance? Maybe she didn't tell you everything because she was afraid that she couldn't count on you." The spoon clanked against the dish as Nicky rose. "You told me once that a family worked to understand each other. She was going to be our family. Dad, what would you have done if you found out after you were married? Would you have made her move out of the house? I'll bet there's a reason why she kept this secret, from you."

Adam shook his head, "Nicky, you're growing up to be a beautiful, smart woman. I don't like it when you use my words against me. However, in this case, the issue is serious and not something I can discuss." He shook his head as Nicky rushed from the room.

AFTER LUNCH, NICKY jogged to Adam's home office. "Dad, is it okay if I go to the mall for a couple hours with my friends?"

"Yes. Just text me their names and numbers and let me know when you get there and when you leave for home."

Adam shut down the computer as his daughter left. He rubbed his eyes and remembered the wardrobe he promised himself to sort through, no time like the present to put that chore behind me.

Upstairs in his bedroom Adam placed a box beside him to store the things he planned to donate. He also had a small plastic tote for keepsakes, which he would put in the attic. He opened the doors to the wooden cabinet. On one side was space to hang delicate clothes. The other side held several drawers and an empty shelf. The little hangers were bare. The only thing left to go through were three drawers.

Adam's hand shook as he pulled out a drawer. "Jesus, give me the strength to do this." He eyed the wardrobe. Katie cherished this chest. Adam hesitantly started to dig into the past.

He pulled out a compartment that housed small boxes of jewelry. With each package, he examined the items. A necklace, a pair of earrings, and a bracelet sparkled in the light. Carefully, Adam placed them on the bed. These will go to Nicky.

The next thing he reached for was a tattered piece of costume jewelry. Adam held the trinket up and thought back to the night he won it for Katie at the State Fair. He took the ornament to his dresser and placed it in his top drawer.

Adam returned to the armoire. A couple scarves went into the donation box and a few other miscellaneous items. He continued working until he reached the last drawer. A partial view told him this area was full of cards and papers.

His eyes ached at the items Katie had treasured. The years' rewound as he examined some of Nicky's elementary projects from school. Colored paper with drawings and verses all neatly banded together. A white ribbon encased the next pile of holiday and birthday cards he'd given Katie throughout the years.

At the bottom of the stack was a red envelope faded with age. He recognized Katie's decorative oversized lettering that she used when she wanted to draw attention to a note. This was something that Katie had meant for him. "Adam" was scribed on the front in flowery writing. His throat grew dry. His chest rose in anticipation as he unfolded the stationary and began to read.

March 16, 2011

My Darling Adam,

If you're reading this, then I'm in heaven. I was fortunate to be your wife. We had some good years together. You have always been my love. I thought I lost you when we had that spat the last year of school. I regret I lost faith in us and went out with my friend's cousin.

The only good that came from that mistake was Nicky. I hope that what I'm about to say doesn't upset you, but I must tell you what I've done. I mailed a letter to Nicky's parental father, Jason Gray. I know I've never mentioned his name, but as I face the end of life, I have a lot of time to think and pray. I felt led to write Jason and tell him about Nicky. I also told him that you were a wonderful dad and I wanted you in her life too.

When you two meet I hope both of you will cherish Nicky and do what is best for her. It's my desire that both of you share a love for her and help her become a well-adjusted woman.

Adam, I also want you to promise you'll move on and find a new love. If I have learned anything these past months, it's been that life is too short for us to fret over things we cannot change.

Open your heart to possibilities. The Lord uses different ways to lead us. Goodbye, my Love.

Adam stood and walked the length of the room as he took in the words. He blinked his eyes to stop the moisture and squinted to try and clear his vision.

Adam held the paper closer as if it could talk. "Well, I don't have to speculate about Jason's reaction." He dropped on to the edge of the bed. The impact of his murmurs stirred a notion. Serena is a Godly woman. I haven't seen her do anything with malice. "Could it all be a coincidence?"

ADAM AND NICKY ARRIVED at church and mingled around the congregation before making their way down the hallway to Nicky's youth class.

"Dad, do you think we'll see Serena?"

"I don't know. She has rotations at the hospital and sometimes works on Sundays." Adam caught himself searching the faces for the woman he stilled loved.

"I hope we do." Nicky headed into her class.

Adam turned toward the main worship area and sat down in an empty pew. After the hymnal singing, he listened as Pastor Bob held up his Bible and spoke.

"Today we're going to discover ways in which the Lord councils us." He waved the book. "It's in His word and through following the path God sets before us that we find happiness. The Lord not only confirms that the way to salvation is by believing, but he wants to show his children the course for their lives."

The minister opened his Bible. "Proverbs 3: 5-6 Trust in the LORD with all thine heart; and lean not unto thine own understanding. In all thy ways acknowledge him, and he shall direct thy paths." Pastor Bob glanced at the congregation. "God will take us to our destiny if we let him. Look at a few of the disciples. These men had no intention of doing the things they did, but they followed God's instruction…"

Adam listened to the church leader seak of Saul, who became Paul and then the minister commented on the things he'd done for God that wasn't what Paul intended to do.

Later, Pastor Bob moved on to other scriptures. "Friends as we depart today, remember Isaiah 42:16. The Lord tells us in that verses that he will make darkness light and crooked things straight. God will not forsake us."

Adam stood for the closing prayer. He made his way into the hall and searched for Nicky. All the while, he studied on a passage the minister brought to his attention and wondered if the Lord tried to guide him.

"Dad, did you see her?" Nicky called out.

"See who?"

"Sereeeena!" Nicky stretched out the word.

Just as Nicky mentioned Serena's name Carole walked by and overheard. "Hi Adam, Serena had to work today. You can catch her at home about four."

Adam smiled. "Thanks, Carole. The Pastor's sermon was interesting today."

"Yes, it was." Carole adjusted her purse strap. "The subject he spoke about reminded me of a time when I felt led by the Lord to invite someone to lunch. We didn't really get alone very well, but I ask her to join me at a restaurant that had just opened. In my mind, I dreaded the date, but I followed through. Because I did what I believed Jesus wanted me to do, the woman received salvation. It turned out that she had many issues and needed a friend who wouldn't judge her. Pastor Bob is right, the Lord sees ahead, and we only notice things for today."

"That's true. We'd better go, have a good afternoon, Carole" Adam motioned for Nicky to move toward the exit.

ADAM DROVE TO A FAVORITE fast-food place he knew Nicky enjoyed. After the burgers were unwrapped, Adam bowed his head.

"Heavenly Father, bless our food and thank you for our Pastor who gives us knowledge to grow in your word, Amen."

Nicky raised her head, "Dad, you've been distracted all morning. What's up?"

"I've been thinking about a couple of things Pastor Bob mentioned."

"Does it have anything to do with Serena?" Nicky dipped a fry in ketchup.

"I suppose it can be applied to my problem. I need to pray about it. Maybe I'll talk to Serena more about that secret."

Nicky's mouth spread wide with expectation, "Dad, you remember when I was mad at Jan and didn't speak to her for a month? She didn't tell me that a new girl made an ugly comment about me in class. I thought about it and realized I'd done the same thing, she's important to me and I wouldn't want to hurt her."

"How could I forget it? You sulked for weeks."

"Yeah, and now you mope around the house all the time. I know you won't tell me what happened, but what if you were in Serena's shoes?"

Adam stopped chewing as he tossed the idea around in his head. He looked at Nicky and smiled. The rest of the meal was eaten while they chatted, light banter and jokes floated across the table. Adam and Nicky went home, and the two of them spent the afternoon watching movies.

THE NEXT WEEK SEEM to linger on. Thursday night Adam got into bed and leaned against the headboard reading. He flipped the pages of the Bible and stopped in the book of Matthew. As Adam read chapter eighteen, he remembered life with Katie, pictured her studying God's word. She liked the parable of the unforgiving servant. Adam closed the Bible. I love Serena. She should have told me. He glanced at his Bible.

"Jesus could I be the unforgiving servant here?" Before Adam lay back, he once again asked for guidance. Nicky's comment about being in Serena's place came to mind. To his surprise, Adam realized he probably would have done the same thing, if a child were involved.

CHAPTER ELEVEN

SERENA PULLED THE LIGHTWEIGHT jacket closer to her body and shivered. She walked through the parking lot to the hospital as the wind whipped around her. An empty Styrofoam cup rolled across her path. She made her way to the elevator and on to the children's wing. The pediatric ward was hustling with activity. Late fall had brought the flu bug and already children were suffering from the season.

Carole watched Serena log on to the computer. "Good morning."

"Hi Carole, you look chipper."

"I am. It's my husband's birthday today, and I plan on taking him out later to celebrate. I enjoy birthday's so much."

"I like them too, even if it means I'm getting older." Serena grinned.

"You don't have anything to worry about you're still young." Carole noticed Serena's finger for the first time in weeks. "Where's your engagement ring?"

Serena sighed, "I gave it back." She watched a wrinkled forehead replace the grin on her co-worker's face. "Carole, I really don't want to talk about it, let's just say I didn't confide in Adam concerning an important situation. When Adam found out he got mad, said he couldn't live with anyone who kept things from him."

Carole looked sympathetically at Serena. She recalled the strained look on Adam's face when they spoke of Serena at church. "Sometimes things have a way of working themselves out. I saw Adam and Nicky in church Sunday. I believe they were looking for you in the crowd. I told Adam you were working."

"Yes, well... I don't know if our misunderstanding can be solved."

Carole picked up a chart and flipped a page. "None of us are perfect. All we can do is our best at the time. I've made choices I regret. The only thing left is to move forward, but if you get a chance to talk to him again, tell him how you feel."

Carole looked at Serena's mouth gaped open ready to speak, and then she quickly interjected. "I know you probably told him that, but a hurt takes time to heal. I'm no expert on men, but the way he acted when I mentioned your name led me to wonder if he really meant what he said about not wanting to get married."

Serena shrugged her shoulders. "I don't know. I love Adam, but I can't say I blame him."

"My mother used to tell me to put yourself in the other person's place and then you'll know what to do." Carole touched Serena's shoulder in understanding and walked away.

SERENA DROVE TO HER house and turned into the driveway, for the hundredth time she recalled the comment Carole made and agreed deep down she knew she'd been mad if situation were reversed.

She walked into her living room. *I should have told Adam from the beginning.* Out of frustration, Serena raised her arms in the air. "It's up to You, Lord."

In the bedroom, Serena changed out of her scrubs into a pair of jeans and a T-shirt. She ambled to the kitchen, made a salad from leftover chicken breasts, and opened a box of gourmet crackers. Serena grabbed a glass and the iced tea from the refrigerator. She placed a container of mixed fruit on the table. As she pulled out a chair, the doorbell rang. She headed to the front door trying to recall if it was time for the paperboy to collect.

"Adam?" Serena's mouth spread in surprise. She stood in the entry and remained motionless.

"Serena, I know I have no right showing up like this after the way I acted, but may I talk to you?"

"Sure, come in." Serena's eyes locked with his, automatically she moved aside. "I was about to eat a quick meal. It's not much, but if you want Chicken salad, you're welcome to join me."

Adam nodded his head, "I'd like that, but maybe another. I need to speak with you, it's important."

"Okay. We'll talk." She headed toward the sofa.

Adam followed. All day, he had mulled over what he wanted to say. He counted back the times he had sought the Lord for answers. Recent thing's folks said to him concerning their personal dilemmas, and regrets seemed to fit his situation, but Pastor Bob's sermon enlightened him the most. Adam knew the Lord often used others to help. "I want us to talk about what happened."

"Adam, I understand, I would have responded the same way." Serena sat on the couch and Adam took a seat beside her.

"Yes, and I probably would handle the information in that letter exactly as you. It was a lot to take in and seeing that note from my late wife was distressful. I should have let you explain things better. I love Nicky and as far as I'm concerned, I've always been her dad. I felt threatened, afraid you would tell her I wasn't her father, and then she'd feel alone in the world." He looked down to the floor. "I still don't understand it all."

"Adam, I told you, I received the letter a few months after Jason passed away. It was a surprise to me too."

"Help me to understand it all." He placed his hand on hers.

Serena nodded. "The letter has several stamped postmarks on it where it traveled to many places. Once it reached me, I read it so many times, grieving for Jason and his child." Serena inhaled a deep breath. "Then after I moved here to be closer to Mom something really strange happened."

"Tell me, please." Adam massaged the top of Serena's hand.

She hung her head. "You'll think I'm crazy," her voice barely audible.

"I came here so we could talk. I want to hear anything you'll tell me. Regardless of our misunderstanding, I still love you. Serena, I know you moved to be closer to the facility your mother is at, but did you know I lived here in Greensboro?"

"No!" She spoke the word with passion. Her eyes searched his face.

"Okay, I'll tell you everything." With a quick motion, she moved her head back and forth. "I'm not off my rocker, Adam."

He smiled, "I would never think that. You're one of the smartest women I know."

Serena mentally prepared herself to tell Adam about Dillon, the child with the message. "Adam, do you believe people can die for a few seconds and experience things we can't explain?"

"You mean the stories about seeing Heaven or life after death experiences?"

"Yes." She shook her head.

"I've heard about those accounts, never knew anyone who experienced it. But who's to say it doesn't happen?"

"Before we met, I was at the hospital and went to check on a child who came in with Cardiac Arrest." Serena started her account and in a cautious dialogue, she retold Adam the things Dillon said and the message he told her.

"I was so shaken, especially after Dillon mentioned my earrings and Jason birthmark... I was in shock."

Adam scratched his head. "That is surreal. It explains a lot."

Serena stood and walked to the fish tank. "All I can do now is promise I'll never mention any of this to Nicky." She watched as the big gold fish swam. "And you know I had the letter out the day you came because I was planning to destroy it."

Adam moved toward Serena. "All of this is a lot to take in, but the Lord works wonders in our lives. One day, when Nicky is grown, perhaps we can tell her together."

He gently turned Serena to face him and embraced her. "I'm tired of questioning the way we met. All I know is I love you and want us to be a family." Adam kissed her, reached in his pocket, and held out the engagement ring. "Serena, please accept this ring back and be my wife? We should be a family, all three of us."

Serena looked hard at the ring. "I do love you, Adam, but I need to think this through."

Adam placed the ring inside her palm. "Pray about us Serena, I'll be waiting." He kissed her and walked out the front door.

Serena stared at the ring and listened as Adam's car pulled onto the main road. *God is this my answer?*

THE NEXT DAY, SERENA called Betsy with the news about the change in events. Her friend listened for ten minutes without speaking.

"And you haven't told him you'll be his wife?" The surprise sounded from her voice.

"No, I haven't spoken to him since yesterday. I guess I'm scared. I came so close to planning our wedding and then all this."

"Hump! Afraid or is your pride getting in the way?"

"My what?" Serena emphasized the words in an irritated voice.

"You're acting like some men do at times. They always think if wronged, things won't be smoothed over. Serena I'm on your side, whatever you do. I just don't want you tossing away a chance for happiness, with the man you love. Think really hard before you do something you'll regret." Betsy paused, "Listen, I gotta go. I'll call you later."

Serena put the phone down and went to the bathroom mocking Betsy. "Is your pride getting in the way?" She turned on the water. *Could Betsy be right?*

ADAM LAUGHED AT A COMEDY show on television. Nicky glanced over at him. "You seem happier today, Dad. What's up?"

"Can't I just enjoy a movie?" Adam's voice sounded amused.

"Dad?" Nicky sounded confident as she waited for an answer.

"Well, I can't offer good news, but I had a long talk with Serena. We hashed out our problem. I gave the ring back to her and she's thinking about our future."

"Dad, that's wonderful!" Nicky voice rose to near squeal. She jumped up, ran to Adam, and grabbed him in a big bear hug.

"Hold on." Adam laughed. "Serena didn't say she would keep the ring, but I hope she's praying about us."

"Oh Dad, I know she will. I'll pray too." Nicky kissed Adam on the cheek. "I'm going to my room. I'll see you in the morning."

SERENA GOT DRESSED for bed. She walked to the computer and decided to look at her messages before she retired for the night. The screen brightened, and she clicked her email icon. The first one she saw was from Adam. She scanned the subject line, "Hello beautiful." Serena examined his greeting telling her he loved and missed her, but wasn't pressuring her.

The next couple of emails were from a shopping site and a medical newsletter subscription. Before she closed down her computer, a chime indicated she had another message. Serena opened the note. The return address showed it belonged to Nicky. Silently she read.

"Hi Serena, Dad told me that you two talked. He never said what happened, and that's okay. Everyone has spats, even Dad and me. I want to ask you to think about us becoming a family. Dad is nutty sometimes, but he really loves you and so do I."

Serena closed her eyes and absorbed the words, and then knelt beside her bed to petition the Lord.

THE WEEKEND PASSED. Monday was Serena's day off from work. She walked into West Gilman Middle School late morning and a familiar voice brought her attention to the end of the hallway.

Serena looked ahead and saw Adam instructing a student on the disadvantages of skipping a class. When He noticed her standing at the end of the hall, Adam excused the teenager, and then walked toward her. "It's good to see you." His eyes lit up and he reached out and took her hand.

"You appear to be busy." She nodded towards the teen as he slipped into a class.

Adam shook his head. "No, the young man is fine, he was just afraid of failing a test so he was going to skip class. I had to point out to him its worse not to take the exam, than to miss

the answers because he didn't try at all."

"I can remember how upset taking exams made me sometimes." She cocked her head sideways. "Do you have a few minutes?"

Nodding, Adam took hold of Serena's elbow as they strolled to his office. He paused at the receptionist desk. "I need some privacy."

"Certainly." The young woman acknowledged his request.

Once Adam and Serena were inside his office he bent down and gave her a kiss.

"For you, I have all the time in the world." Serena blushed and opened her hand to reveal the engagement ring. "I want to become Mrs. Adam Knox. Will you put the ring back on my finger?"

"If we weren't in school, I'd pick you up, twirl you around, and kiss you senseless." Adam smiled, his eyes dance with excitement. He took the ring and reached for her hand. "Will you

marry me and be my forever."

"Oh, yes." She nodded and her musical giggle filled the air.

"I will marry you."

Adam leaned over and kissed her again. This time the kiss lingered. Serena pressed her hand gently on his chest and he pulled away. "It's good we're in a public place. Besides, I'm going to need all my wits to arrange a wedding in five weeks. Thank goodness I forgot to cancel most of the arrangements."

She held her hand up and surveyed the ring. "Now, for the next reason I stopped by. What are you and Nicky doing for Thanksgiving?"

"We usually make the best of the holiday. Nicky likes to fix the Turkey and leave me with the rest of the side dishes. What did you have in mind?"

"Why don't the two of you come over to my condominium for dinner? I'll have to work during the day, but we can eat about six."

Adam licked his lips in anticipation. "Sounds good, but Nicky and I can do the cooking at our place, you can join us there since you have to work."

Serena turned her head contemplating. "I must admit that is tempting, how about I make some pies? "Great, I'll see you on Thursday."

"I'd better go and let you get back to work. Tell Nicky I'll see her in a few days." Serena turned to walk away.

Adam reached for her. "I love you." He hugged her and whispered in her ear. "I'm so happy we're going to be a family. I can't wait until we get married. I can hold you in my arms all night."

CHAPTER TWELVE

WEDNESDAY SERENA FINISHED her morning rounds and went to the break room. Carole was throwing a Granola wrapper away.

"Serena, you're all smiles today."

"I guess I am." She held up her hand.

"You have the ring back on. I suppose that means you and Adam talked through the problems."

"It does, the wedding is still set for the end of December. I hope you'll come."

"I'll be there" Carole took Serena's hand and eyed the ring.

"The Lord is good. I prayed you'd work things out."

"I appreciate it."

ON THANKSGIVING, SERENA finished her workday and drove to Adam's house.

The sound of the doorbell rang.

"Dad she's here," Nicky shouted.

"Go let her in while I pull the sweet potatoes out of the oven."

Nicky jogged to the front door and swung it open. "Man, I'm glad to see you. I prayed that you and Dad would get back together." She embraced Serena.

Serena chuckled, "There were many people praying. Now that the wedding is back on we have a lot to do in a month's time."

Serena walked toward the dining room. Nicky matched her steps. "Don't worry, we can do it, I'll help with everything."

"I know you will. Thanks." Serena put her arm around Nicky,

The dining room table held all the trimmings for a Thanksgiving feast. Serena inhaled the aroma of the turkey as she scanned the dishes of potatoes, stuffing, and a green bean casserole. She laughed at the huge bowl of macaroni and cheese sitting in the middle of the table.

"Adam, it looks like you and Nicky have been cooking all day."

Adam stood beside her and embraced her in a hug. "It's nothing, my lady." He kissed her. "Are we all ready?" Adam pulled out a chair for Serena and then one for Nicky.

"It looks good, both of you may spoil me."

Nicky took a seat on the other side of the table. "It's okay, we don't mind."

"Let's say a blessing." Adam sat at the head of the table and reached for Serena and Nicky's hand. "Lord, as we celebrate this holiday, we come to you in humbleness. Thank you for bringing us together. Bless this wonderful food set before us and keep us in your will. Serena and I especially thank you for the Angels that guided us to become a family. Amen."

Adam lifted his head and smiled at Serena. They shared an understanding look.

As they dished out food, talk filled the room. Adam chewed his turkey and grinned while he listened to the females chat about wedding plans.

"Serena, do you want me to call the caterers tomorrow and make sure everything is ready for December twenty-eight?" Nicky reached for the rolls.

"Serena hesitated for a second. Giving Nicky's age she wondered if the teenage could handle it.

"That would be a big help, but I need to go there anyway. Would you confirm things with the florist? You know all the flower arrangements we'll be using."

Adam added, "I'll speak with Pastor Bob to double check the accommodations for the church and the banquet hall."

"Dad, I spoke with Jan's Mom and she said I could spend a few days with them if you go on a honeymoon. Are you going away?"

Adam put down his napkin. "Actually, I had already asked her to watch you." They both laughed.

He turned his attention to Serena. "I know we haven't talked about a honeymoon, but if you can get some time off, we could take a cruise. I have some pamphlets you can look at. The cruise director assured me she could find us a nice ship heading to the Bahamas."

"I'd like that. I scheduled time off and Carole also said she could work a couple days for me."

Nicky screeched with joy. "That sounds like fun. I wish I could go."

Adam's eyes got wide. "No, not this time, but Serena and I will take you for your sixteenth birthday."

Serena laid her fork down and looked at Adam and Nicky.

"I would like to ask both of you something."

"Anything, you know that." Adam sat his beverage down.

"Remember I mentioned my mother living in an assisted living facility a short distance from here." Serena looked at Adam and watched him nod his head. "I was wondering if all of us could visit her before the wedding. I'd like Mom to meet you." She glanced at Adam and then Nicky.

Adam turned his attention to Nicky. "I'm anxious to get to know my future mother-in-law. What do you think Nicky?"

Before Nicky could respond Serena touched Nicky's hand and added, "My mother has started to show signs of Alzheimer's. Don't think anything about it if she says the same thing several times, her memory is failing."

Nicky grinned at Serena. "I know about Alzheimer's; my friend's grandmother has the illness. We've talk about it."

"Is Saturday a good time?" Serena scanned both faces as they nodded.

After the meal Nicky headed to her room. Serena helped clean the kitchen while Adam fixed several carryout containers.

"I'm glad you came over." He moved closer, circled Serena in his arms and felt her snuggle into his embrace.

"I wouldn't have missed it. I enjoy having a family dinner with you and Nicky."

"Soon it will be every night."

Adam kissed her lightly and walked a few steps to the counter. "I have your dinner for the next few days." He held a bag.

"My goodness, thanks Adam I'll enjoy the meals after work." Serena took the bag.

"Want to go sit on the couch for a while?"

"Sure, I'd like that."

They walked into the living area and took a seat. Adam put his arm over her shoulder. "I honestly can't see my life without you."

"I don't want to imagine being away from you either." Time clicked by as they talked. Serena lifted her head from its resting spot, on Adam's shoulder. "I need to go, it's getting late."

At the door Serena said goodnight and moved deeper into his embrace. "I love you so much. I never thought I could feel this way again."

SATURDAY SERENA CALLED Adam and told him she was on her way to his house.

"Good, do we have time to stop for breakfast before we visit your mom? Nicky wants pancakes."

"Sure. Mountain Laurel is at the Winston Salem exit. It's only thirty minutes from here."

She pulled into the driveway and Nicky jogged to the car followed by Adam. They stopped at Waffle Home for pancakes.

As they got out of the car Nicky's added. "I want blueberry."

Adam chuckled, "Yes, I figured that." He smiled at Serena.

"She would live off those things if I let her."

"Sounds good," Serena agreed with Nicky while they headed toward the entrance of the restaurant.

After breakfast, Serena headed to I-85, took the exit, and after five miles, veered into the parking lot of Mountain Laurel Assisted Living. She located a parking spot. All three of them strolled down the sidewalk passed the huge flowerpots filled with fall colors.

Adam and Nicky followed Serena under the covered patio flanked by rockers. Adam held the door for Serena and Nicky as they walked down the corridor.

Serena greeted the nurse at the desk and turned left going to the last door. She knocked.

"Come in," A gentle voice spoke.

Serena stepped in the room and glided to her mother's side. Her mother smiled and pulled her close. "It's so good to see you." She released her daughter.

Serena reached for Nicky. "Mom, this is Nicky and Adam Knox, remember I told you Adam and I are getting married?"

Adam reached his hand toward Serena's mom. "Pleased, Ms. Tilley."

The woman squinted at Adam. "Shucks, you need to call me Emma. Come here." Her hand extended to both of them. First, her focus was on Nicky, "You sure are a pretty young lady." Emma hugged the teenager and then pulled Adam closer for a greeting.

The morning flew by and went better than expected. Her mom was having a good day and only got confused a few times. Nicky cupped her hand around the phone as she shared pictures and showed off Serena's gown for Ms. Tilley to see.

"Oh my, that's a pretty dress, now when are you getting married?"

Serena smiled and patted her mother's hand announcing the date again, as she had for several days. "December twenty-eight."

Emma turned her attention to Adam. "Where do you work?"

"I'm the principal for South Gilman Middle School. That's how Serena and I met. She came to talk to the class about nursing." Adam remembered speaking the same sentences when he first arrived.

"Well, it worked out the way God intended." Emma looked at her daughter and the others. "Maybe all of you needed to be a family."

As Emma's words penetrated the room, Serena and Adam gazed at each other, silently remembering the secret they shared.

Serena stood, "I couldn't be happier than to become part of the Knox family." She turned and eyed the clock beside the chair. "We better go. Mom, I'll be back mid-week. Serena rose and embraced her mother

Nicky turned off the game she was playing on her phone and walked over to Emma. "I'm glad I got to come and spend the day with you."

"Well, I know you have plenty of things to do." She hugged Nicky, "But it was wonderful.

Emma wheeled her chair toward Adam. "You'll make Serena happy. I know you will."

"I'm certainly going to try and I'm happy to be part of your family, Emma." He bent and held her hand.

DECEMBER WAS A FLURRY of activity. During the middle of the month, they decorated a Christmas tree at Adam and Nicky's house.

"Are you sure you don't want to put out ornaments and Christmas stuff at you apartment, Serena?" Nicky questioned as she strung lights.

"No, I'm packing and getting ready to move in with you guys. It would only make more work for me. I'll enjoy the holiday's here."

Adam stepped close and kissed Serena on the cheek. "I have a friend who is going to help me move your belongings when we get back from our honeymoon."

THE WEEK BEFORE CHRISTMAS, Serena, Adam and Nicky went to Salvation's Door to watch a theatrical production of The Birth of Jesus. The church was full of people anticipating the story of Mary and Joseph.

Nicky sat between Adam and Serena. "I'm glad we came to the church play. I remember years ago it used to be tradition with us." She dropped her voice, "when Mom was alive."

"Yes, it did." Adam turned to Serena. "At one time Katie and I were very active in church. She loved all the performances and musicals."

He put his arm over the pew and rubbed Nicky's shoulder. "It's my fault for letting Nicky and I lose sight of the important things."

Serena gently turned Nicky's face to her. "I think that is a wonderful custom for any family to have. Maybe we can honor your mother by continuing to attend the events she enjoyed so much and Nicky, you can talk about your mother anytime. I want to know all about her."

CHRISTMAS MORNING CAME and Serena arrived at the Knox house early. Adam greeted her at the door, "Merry Christmas."

Serena hugged Adam and saw Nicky sitting Indian style beside the tree, "Merry Christmas everyone. Adam my presents are in the car will you get them?" "Sure." He slid on his coat.

"Serena, look Dad got me a new phone."

She smiled at Nicky. "I'll be right back to look at your gift." Serena took her dinner to the kitchen and returned to examine the icons on the touch screen. "That's neat. It has just about anything you'd need."

"Here we go." Adam closed the door with his foot as he balanced packages in his arms.

All three of them sat in a circle and handed out gifts. Nicky tore open one of the packages Serena gave her, and held up a pair of the latest style jeans, along with a matching sweater and jacket. She eye a small box wrapped in bright red. Nicky ripped the paper off and pulled out a chain with a gold cherub. The figure had outstretched wings and an etching on the front of the angel's gown, Nicky read aloud. "Your guardian angel is with you and awaits you in Heaven." The teenager stared at the necklace as a tear gathered on her eyelash.

Serena hugged Nicky, "Your mom will forever be a part of your life, and I'll always respect her as your mother. She loved you very much."

"Thank you, it's beautiful. I do miss Mom, but I'm glad you and Daddy found each other."

"Nicky, Serena, and I had help in becoming a family." Adam added, "Angels are wonderful. Here Serena, open one of my gifts."

Serena grinned and took the present Adam handed her. She opened the green and blue snowman paper to revel a square container. She picked up a bracelet and admired the charms dangling from it.

Adam pointed to the round bangle. The lady at the jewelry store told me you can get different trinkets. I chose these along with the nurse's charm. Nicky picked out the angel."

Nicky held up her necklace and interjected, "great minds think alike. She's pretty, just like my guardian."

Serena grinned. "I love it, thank you."

Adam touched the other adornments. This heart signifies my love and the wedding bell means I'll honor you forever."

"Adam, I'll wear it all the time." She leaned over and kissed him. "I'm afraid I didn't do as good picking out your gift, but I hope you'll enjoy it." She laid a long box on his lap.

Adam lifted his eyebrow at the long flat gift. "A tie?" amusement rang in his tone. He removed the lid from the box and pulled out a watch. "Serena, this is a nice timepiece. You noticed the dilapidated band on mine." He glanced at his wrist.

"I did, but it's not only something to tell time with. Look on the back."

Adam tuned over the dial and read the engraving. "To my

love, God gave us a life together that I'll cherish forever."

He looked at his fiancé. "It's more than I wanted. Your love is all I need." Adam kissed Serena.

Nicky shook her head. "Okay you two, stop the slobbering. We have a few more things to unwrap."

After opening all the gifts, Nicky grabbed her packages and headed to the stairs. "I'll be back in a little bit. I'm going to try on my jeans."

Adam watched his daughter bound the steps, two at a time. "And text her friend from her new phone, no doubt." He reached for Serena's hand. "I have something to show you."

Adam led her to the hall closet and took an envelope out of his jacket. "I wanted to show this to you days ago, but we've been busy." He handed the note to her. "Please, read it."

Serena opened the folded paper and stared at the same kind of handwriting she'd seen on Jason's letter from Katie. Adam stood quietly and waited for her to take in all the words on the page.

After several seconds, she gave the envelope back. "Wow, so you have one too."

"Yes, but I didn't know it was in the house. It was in antique chest Katie had. I only found it a couple weeks ago."

That's why you understand my letter." Serena smiled. "In both her letters, Katie mentioned that the Lord works in different ways. I recall the things that the little boy told me. I have

to believe it was God's guidance."

Adam moved closer, "I know. I stepped away from God for a time, but he used you to bring me back to the fold and I know the Lord works out other problems, if we listen to his leading." He spoke in a low tone. "Do you still have the letter Katie wrote to Jason?"

"Yes, I packed it away in the box."

Adam put the envelope back in his pocket. "We'll keep both of them. One day we'll tell Nicky about this, and the letters will be a comfort to her."

"Adam, in the years to come I believe God will lead us to do what is needed. For now, Nicky has you and me to give her love, anything more will confuse her, one day she'll be grown."

Later that day everyone sat down to a holiday feast. Chatter filled the air about the New Year, and beginning a life together as a family.

Afterward they took pie to the TV room and watched a heartwarming movie about a country singer stranded in a small town on Christmas Eve. The credits rolled across the screen, Serena eyed Adam and Nicky. "As much as I hate to go, I need to leave. I want to go spend the rest of the evening with Mom" She hugged both of them and gathered her purse and gifts.

"Thanks for the wonderful day, I love my gifts."

Adam and Nicky followed Serena to the door. "I'll see you day after tomorrow. I'm spending the night at your house, right." Nicky hugged her.

Serena nodded her head. "Betsy and Keith are arriving and Adam will drop you off. We have hair appointment's early Friday morning."

"Okay." Nicky's attention went to the phone as she headed back upstairs.

Adam walked Serena to her car. "I love you." He circled his arms around her and kissed her. Adam took hold of the door after Serena scooted inside. "Keith will be staying over here. I believe he is riding back with me when I bring Nicky by."

"That's what I'm told. I'll ride to the church with Betsy, that way we each have our own cars when the wedding is over. Until then my darling," Adam's lips covered hers with a promise of his devotion.

CHAPTER THIRTEEN

KEITH AND BETSY STEPPED inside. Keith carried his wife's suitcase to the extra bedroom. Serena called after him. "I have sub are ready. I hope you're hungry."

"Are you kidding? The man eats all the time. I don't know where he gets his appetite." Betsy followed Serena to the kitchen. "Are you ready for the big day?"

"Yes, I am. Your and Nicky's dresses are hanging in the bedrooms."

Keith's rough voice broke into the conversation. "Okay, let's eat."

Seated at the table, each with a sub and potato chips, Keith grabbed the sandwich. "When is Adam coming?"

"He should be dropping Nicky by in about an hour. He wanted to treat her to a special dinner, before the wedding."

Betsy filled the bun with lettuce. "Did you tell me you're going to Paradise Island, in the Bahamas for your honeymoon?"

"Yes, I read a little about it on the brochure and it says the island is pure euphoria." Serena put her fingers up and made quotation marks in the air.

"I know you're going have fun." Betsy took a bite of the sandwich. "Is your mother coming to the wedding?"

Serena took a swallow of her beverage. "No, she can't. She has a stomach virus. The sickness has drained all her energy. I'm going to take her a DVD of the ceremony when we get back from our honeymoon."

The three of them discussed the pending marriage, work, and Serena's honeymoon destination.

The sound of scuffling at the door brought a huge grin to Serena's face. "That must be Nicky." She let the teenager inside and took the overnight from Adam.

"Hi Keith," Adam pulled his bride close to his side. "Are you ready to get away from the women for a night?"

Keith grinned and kissed Betsy on the cheek. "Sure, there are only so many times a guy can listen to the pros and cons of wearing an off-the-shoulder dress. I'll get my bag from the car and meet you outside."

Adam laughed, "Nicky, I'll see you tomorrow honey." "Okay, Dad." She walked over and hugged him.

Adam kissed Nicky on the cheek and turned, facing Betsy and his daughter, "will you ladies excuse me a moment. I need to say good bye to my bride."

Adam held Serena's hand and guided her to the hallway. "I can't wait until tomorrow afternoon. Serena, you've made me a very happy man." Adam laid his hand on her neck and bent down enclosing her mouth with his.

Serena returned the embrace. She let desire wash over her as their lips touched in a deep embrace. Finally, she moved out of his arms. "Adam, you better go. Tomorrow we will be man and wife."

"I can't wait. I'll have you in my arms forever." He stepped out into the night.

TUNES FROM THE SONG "You light up my Life," flowed from the piano throughout the church. Nicky hugged Serena. "I'm so happy that we're going to be a family."

Betsy clicked a picture. "Serena, you look beautiful. I hear the music changing, it's time."

Adam leaned back on his heels and watched his daughter and the matron of honor slowly make their way to the front.

The music changed to the traditional part as the bride slowly glided down the aisle. Adam's heart beat faster with each measured step she took. He gazed the length of her body. The ivory gown fitted close to her waist, the neckline just low enough to make him admire her womanly figure. As she approached, Adam noticed the intricate beaded jacket that covered her shoulders.

The minister waited for Serena to reach Adam. They stood side by side facing him. "Today we're gathered together to join Serena Gray and Adam Knox in matrimony."

Serena's mouth went dry while she took in every word. As much as she enjoyed weddings, she was eager for Pastor Bob to pronounce them man and wife.

A quick thought flashed in her mind of a time when she'd never imagined having a spouse again. Here I stand with the other love of my life. The pastor asked her if she took Adam as her husband.

She glanced at Adam and spoke a resounding, "I do."

Adam moved closer to Serena and placed the ring on her finger. He stared into her eyes and grinned nervously while he repeated the vows, quickly adding his confirmation to love and honor her forever.

Pastor Bob announced, "You may kiss the bride."

Adam gazed into her eyes and their lips met in the symbolic fashion to seal the union, then everyone clapped.

"Friends and family as we celebrate the marriage of Adam and Serena, let's remember Ecclesiastes 9-12." The pastor opened his Bible and read. "'wo are better than one; because they have a good reward for their labour. For if they fall, the one will lift up his fellow: but woe to him that is alone when he falleth; for he hath not another to help him up. Again, if two lie together, then they have heat: but how can one be warm alone? And if one prevail against him, two shall withstand him; and a threefold cord is not quickly broken.'"

He closed the black leather-bound book and joyfully announced. "I give you Mr. and Mrs. Adam Knox. May, the Lord always be their guide."

The newlyweds made their way down the aisle and outside. Adam and Serena dodged birdseed that the guests tossed into the air, while they rushed across the street where the reception awaited.

"The wedding was beautiful." Betsy greeted them at the door of the fellowship building.

"It was, but I thought it would never get here." Adam nodded.

Serena admired her husband in his three-piece navy-blue tuxedo. She gazed at the way his suit fitted against his well-toned chest. The tie matched the wedding colors with ivory and gold.

Adam clasped Serena's hand and along with Nicky, they greeted guest and thank everyone for coming.

With the crystal cleared away. Adam and Serena stood at the table in front of the four-tiered cake. The ivory and gold icing formed flowers on the side. A plastic bride and groom holding hands posed on the top. They cut the cake. The guest clapped as the newlyweds fed each other a bite of the dessert.

Adam, Serena, and Nicky sat at the table of honor. Adam watched the time, quietly counting down the hours until he and Serena could be alone in their honeymoon cabin on the ship.

The band requested the newlyweds to lead the dance. Adam strolled with his bride to the middle of the room and took her in his arms as the music started. Serena swayed and listened to Adam's baritone voice repeating the lyrics, "It was no accident, me finding you. Someone had a hand in it, long before we ever knew." He kissed her ear, and she cuddled into his body.

Music for a fast dance played and Adam seized the moment. "Serena, let's go and change into our travel clothes. We should get to the airport." He took her hand and moved toward the front.

Thirty minutes later, Serena glanced at the women gathered around. She tossed the arrangement in the air and laughed along with the preacher's daughter who caught the bouquet.

"I'll call you in a week Betsy." Serena waved as they made their way to where Nicky stood.

"Dad, is it time for you to go?"

Adam hugged Nicky and whispered, "Yes, we need to get to the airport terminal. You listen to Jan's mother while we're gone."

"I will. Have fun on your honeymoon and bring me back a souvenir. I love you guys." Nicky hugged them.

THE PLANE LANDED. A shuttle bus took them to the ship and Serena and Adam boarded the cruiser. With the luggage secured, they followed the instructions on the information packet and moved through the crowded hall to their room.

Serena walked into the room and noticed the welcome towels made into swans sitting on the silk crimson coverlet. She took a few steps toward the door that led to the balcony. "This is beautiful. I can't wait until we're at sea and can view the gorgeous Island. We can sip fruit drinks on the balcony, Adam. It's lovely."

"It certainly is a nice suite. The space is large, considering we're on a cruise." Adam worked to unpack his carryall.

Serena put a few of her toiletries from her tote bag in a nearby drawer and surveyed the accommodations. The bed stood in the middle of the space. A red skirt dressed the bottom of the sleeping unit. One side of the room featured shelves, closet, and drawers. The other side of the cabin held a nook with a desk and the bathroom entrance.

Serena picked out her nighttime ensemble and headed to the shower. The ship hadn't yet departed so Adam sat on the bed and sent a text message to Nicky telling her they were on their way out to sea.

Serena returned and saw her husband taking keys and change out of his pants pockets. He quickly moved to her side. His eyes went the length of her body as he kissed her. "You're beautiful Mrs. Knox."

Serena grinned and touched the strap of her lingerie, the sheer material ending midway above her knees. "Why, Mr. Knox, I didn't think you'd notice?" She batted her eyes and mimicked a southern belle.

"My darling, I noticed a long time ago and now, I get to enjoy every inch of the scenery." He slipped his finger under her strap, ran his hand over her bare shoulder, and then scooped her in his arms, laying her on the crimson bed cover. Adam's gentle kiss grew deeper with love and desire for his wife.

THE HONEYMOON CRUISE was ending. Serena stood on the deck, scanned the horizon, and spoke softly. "Lord, I thank you for leading me to Adam. I have a second chance with love, and I promise to make every minute count."

She tilted her head to heaven and watched as a big white cloud made in the formation of an angel, slowly moved across the sky.

The End

Dear Readers,

I hope you enjoyed Serena's story. Although Postmarked Ever After is fiction, I'm sure we have all been touched by the loss of a love one. Just like Serena and Adam, it is with God's grace that we overcome and move forward.

Here is Serena's homemade Macaroni and Cheese recipe. If you like mac and cheese you'll enjoy this recipe.

2 cups macaroni (uncooked)

1/4 cups cheddar cheese (shredded)

eggs

2 1/2 cups milk

1/4 teaspoon pepper

1-teaspoon salt

Paprika

Directions: Cook macaroni until soft.

Use a large casserole dish. Place a thin layer of macaroni on the bottom, and spread the cheese over the layer, repeat this process using all of the macaroni and cheese. You will have several layers.

Mix salt, pepper, eggs and milk together. Pour on top of the layered macaroni & cheese. Sprinkle with paprika and cover with foil. Place in oven and bake in a 350 degrees oven for 45 minutes.

Don't miss out!

Visit the website below and you can sign up to receive emails whenever Mary L Ball publishes a new book. There's no charge and no obligation.

https://books2read.com/r/B-A-MPLD-RNBL

BOOKS 2 READ

Connecting independent readers to independent writers.